D1825689

# A VICARAGE IN THE BLITZ

The Wartime Letters of Molly Rich
London 1940-1944

*With illustrations by Anthea Craigmyle*

*For Molly and Otto*

First published in 2013 Balloon View Ltd, Kent, TN26 2DD
Copyright © Anthea Craigmyle 2013.

ISBN: 978-1-907798-38-2

All rights reserved. No part of this publication may be reproduced, stored,
or transmitted in any form, or by any means, electronic, mechanical or
photocopying, recording or otherwise, without the express written
permission of the publisher.

Edited by Cynthia Penney.
Designed by Teresa Monachino.
Printed and bound in Britain by Emtone Press, Bath.

*Molly Rich (1899-1974) was born in London to
Major R M Richardson and his wife Helen, née Croft.
She married the Rev Edward Rich in 1927 and the
family came to St Nicholas Chiswick in 1934.*

# INTRODUCTION

The letters of Molly Rich, my mother, were written to Otto, a 20-year-old refugee from Vienna who came to live with us at Chiswick Vicarage early in 1939 and quickly became part of the family. Fourteen months later, as Hitler invaded Europe, Otto was arrested as an Enemy Alien and sent to internment camps in England and then Australia. Released fourteen months after his arrest, Otto joined the Pioneer Corps (a military auxiliary) and then the Army, serving in England, France and Germany as the Allies fought to victory.

Much loved by us four children, Otto was considered a fifth child by our mother, who wrote to him throughout the war. After Molly's death in 1974, I was lunching with Otto and his wife when he told me he still had all her letters. I was greatly excited, as Molly was a natural communicator, writing with charm and energy to her children away at school, her mother in Hertfordshire, her sisters in Kenya and extended family in Trinidad and America. I did not realise the full power of her gift, however, until Otto handed me six boxes of correspondence and said in his gentle, deep voice, "These letters kept me alive".

Molly had typed or handwritten over six hundred letters, filling every inch of wartime paper. She described the life of an ordinary family living in a part of London that suffered badly during the Blitz. The topics are largely domestic because of wartime censorship and because Molly had little time for anything but work in a household of 14 people, three dogs, two cats and a canary, not to mention chickens and rabbits.

Molly's husband, my father, was Edward Rich ('Teddy' or 'Uncle E'), vicar of St Nicholas, then a parish of 11,000 people, many of them very poor. Molly and Edward had four children: Helen, Lawrence, Patience and me, the youngest, aged from twelve to six in 1940. Edward's curate, Fred Wright, had a bed-sit arrangement on the top floor with his white-and-tan spaniel, Tasher. The remaining ten bedrooms spilled over with refugees from Estonia, Austria,

Germany and Belgium, evacuees from bombed-out houses in the neighbourhood and London's East End, and visiting family and friends. Alice, the untalented cook who was Molly's only servant, left in 1940. There was one indoor lavatory.

Molly was not a natural housekeeper. Brought up in a country house, she was sent at 16 to a domestic college and taught to use a flat iron and to cook and sew. Life at the Vicarage was wildly chaotic. While trying to keep the household clean and clothed and doing a great deal of parish work, our mother dug the lawn to grow vegetables, created an air-raid shelter in the cellar and helped the Women's Voluntary Service and the Mothers' Union, often after a long night of fire-watching. She managed all the cooking with wartime rations ("I can now conjure meals from air") and did the shopping on an old racing bike. As no one ever thought to reverse the handlebars, she rode bent over while balancing string bags that trailed to the ground. She would attempt to do the housework each morning by 6 am, long before we were awake, then take a cup of tea to my father before he left for morning service. She lit fires, fought battles with mice and knitted socks for all of us very rapidly on four needles.

The Vicarage, part Caroline, part Victorian, was considered old-fashioned even then. The cavernous kitchen and scullery with a four-foot stone sink were at the end of a flagged corridor. A small, very black gas oven crouched in the darkest corner. We often had meals in the kitchen at two six-foot tables placed end to end. The drawing room upstairs overlooked the river, a beautiful room with a grand piano played wonderfully by Teddy and Helen. My father's study was a haven of peace, with a red Turkey carpet and walls lined with books and prints of church luminaries.

There was a wide garden all round the house, surrounded by an old brick wall. At the north end grew three great elm trees. A fig tree of vast height stood by the west wall, forming a green canopy that reached to the ground. The wall on the south side overlooked Chiswick Mall, the green and beyond that, the great rolling Thames. The wall was the focus of our childhood as it was a perfect lookout post. The world went on below and beyond it.

*The garden wall of the Vicarage was a perfect lookout post for Molly's children.*

Our playground was the river and, at low tide, the island (Chiswick Eyot), the graveyards, the old shipyards of Church Wharf and the extensive grounds of Chiswick House. For a small child life was exciting and sometimes dangerous. We were left entirely to our own devices.

Lawrence led the way for exploration and feats of prowess, daring and skill. He was a member of 'the big boys' gang', a collection of the wilder neighbouring children. On winter nights before the blackout restrictions, the boys would leap up the Mall waving sticks bound with flaming rags. As they whooped and yelled, Patience and I felt a deep sense of the unfairness of having been born girls. The culmination of the boys' adventures was blowing up the outside loo (sacrosanct for our father's use) with a firework. This catastrophe nearly ended the gang's existence.

Helen did not play with us. Although only six years older, she seemed a generation apart. She didn't storm about the garden and climb walls and trees, but had a feminine life of sweetness in a more grown-up world.

*Anthea in 1940.*

At the outbreak of war, Helen and Lawrence were at boarding school. Patience and I were evacuated from Chiswick to our maternal grandmother in Hertfordshire and attended Ware Grammar School, walking each day the couple of miles from her house over the fields to Ware. Molly sometimes joined us during our holidays and some of her letters are written from 'Amwell Bury'.

As a country girl, Molly found London in the early '30s a dark and strange environment, though she liked to recall that on the night of her arrival at the Vicarage, the owls living in the church tower flew about her head and seemed to hoot a welcome. Molly came to love the Vicarage and indeed London itself and the many people she encountered. She became a mother not only to Otto but also to all her refugees and evacuees and a support and friend to neighbours, the bombed-out and anyone else in need. Molly had honey-coloured hair and hazel eyes. She was very shy but full of energy and kindness. She had time for everyone. And, somehow, she found the time to write.

ANTHEA CRAIGMYLE, CHISWICK, 2013

*St Nicholas church and the Vicarage at low tide c. 1925.*
*(Courtesy of Local Studies Collection, Chiswick Library)*

# MAP OF CHISWICK 1940

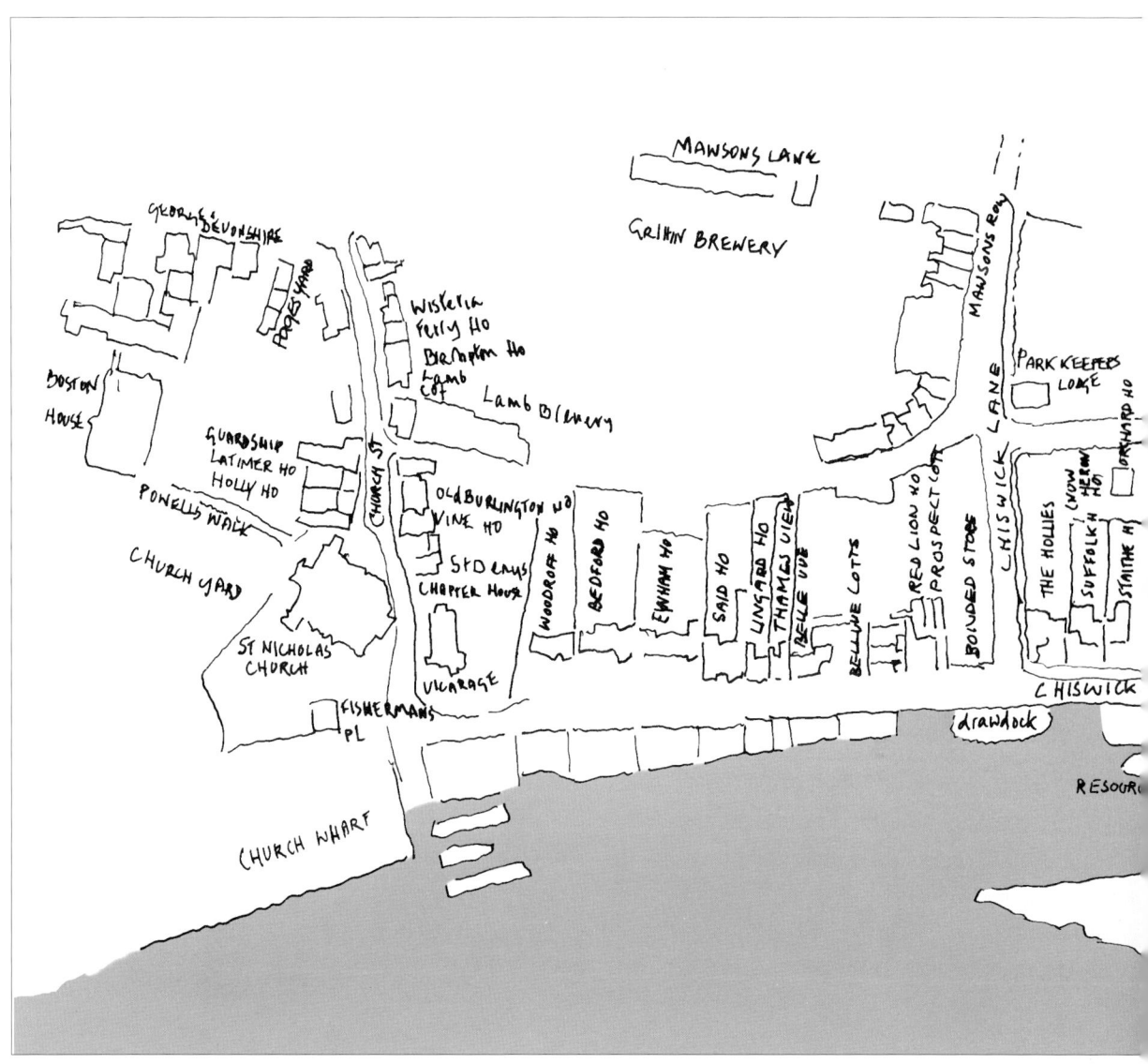

*The Rich family in 1940.*

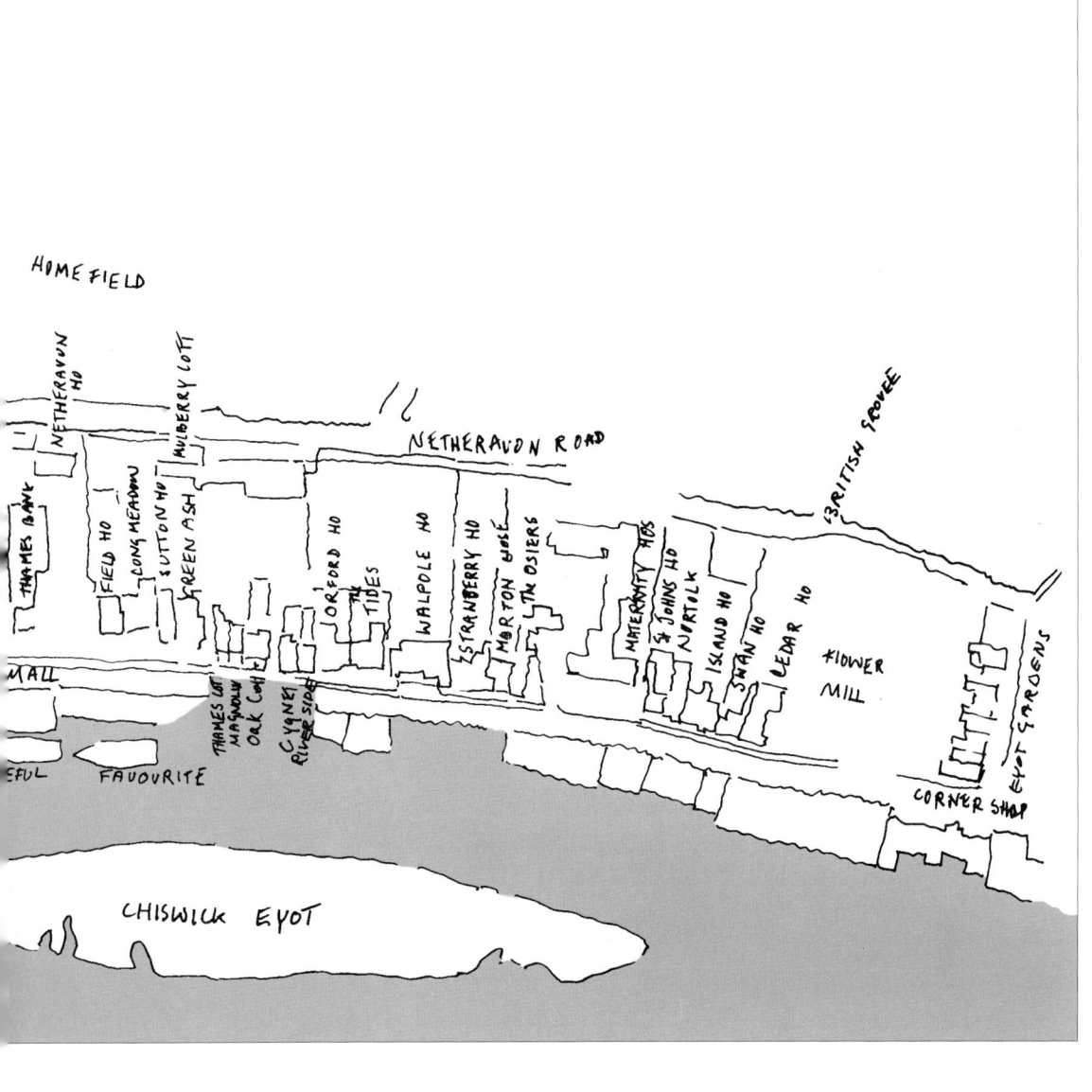

HOMEFIELD

NETHERAVON HO

THAMES BANK

FIELD HO

LONG MEADOW

SUTTON HO

MULBERRY LOTT

GREEN ASH

NETHERAVON ROAD

ORFORD HO

THE TIDES

WALPOLE HO

STRAWBERRY HO

MORTON HOSÉ

THE OSIERS

BRITISH GROVE

MATERNITY HOS

ST JOHNS HO

NORFOLK

ISLAND HO

SWAN HO

CEDAR HO

FLOWER MILL

EYOT GARDENS

MALL

THAMES COTT

MAGNOLIA

OAK COTT

CYGNET

RIVER SIDE

EFUL

FAVOURITE

CORNER SHOP

CHISWICK EYOT

*Edward Rich (centre); Fred Wright (curate) on his right; Sister Alethe of St Denys; church wardens Walter Elwell and Bert Townsend and the choir and other parish helpers.*

# MOLLY'S FAMILY, FRIENDS AND NEIGHBOURS

## AT THE VICARAGE IN 1940

**Molly Rich**, the author of these letters, was 41 years old in 1940.

**Edward Rich**, Molly's husband and the vicar of St Nicholas, was also called 'Uncle Edward' or 'Teddy'. He was 44.

**Helen**, aged 12, the eldest of the four Rich children, was at Abingdon School in Oxfordshire.

**Lawrence**, aged 10, attended Brackley School in Northamptonshire.

**Patience** and **Anthea**, 'the little girls', were 8 and 6, respectively and attended Ware Grammar School.

**Bonzo**, also called Bonny, was the family rough--haired Dachshund.

**Dinah** was the family's perpetually pregnant black Manx cat.

**Alice**, a servant, lived in a room off the kitchen and left early in 1940, to Molly's relief. She wrote and visited occasionally, hoping to return.

**Fred Wright** was Edward's curate. He had a room on the top floor with his spaniel, **Tasher**, until leaving the parish in February 1942.

**Miss Coverley**, a bombed-out neighbour, lodged at the Vicarage with her cat and canary from September 1940 to April 1944.

**Gem Coverley**, niece of Miss Coverley, was a young nurse in training. She stayed at the Vicarage on her days off from a London hospital.

**'The Belgians'** was a term Molly used to describe refugees from Belgium billeted in Chiswick. Living at the Vicarage were the Leonards: **'Madame'**, the mother; daughter **Denese**; and two babies, **Albert** and **Marie Rose**. They moved out in July 1940 but remained nearby.

**Mr** and **Mrs Adams** and their daughter and son-in-law, **the Morleys**, were evacuees from London's heavily bombed East End. The two couples were billeted at the Vicarage with their dog, **Micky**, from September 1940 to March 1941.

## AT THE VICARAGE LATER IN THE WAR

Molly befriended and sheltered over 20 young refugees from Germany, Austria and enemy-occupied countries. Six are mentioned in the published letters.

**Myra**, Otto's sister, left Vienna in 1938 and worked as a housemaid near London. Later she found work at a leather goods firm and stayed at the Vicarage from February to December 1941 before moving to a rooming house.

**Ilse** was from Germany. She arrived at the Vicarage in May 1941 and worked for a milliner.

**Irene** was born in Estonia. She was at a school in England when the Soviets took over her country in June 1940. After finishing her studies, she joined the Rich family in July 1941 and worked first for the Girl Guides and then at the BBC.

**Hans** was born in Germany. He was at a school in Wells when the war started and stayed in England to study engineering. He spent 10 days of his summer holiday at the Vicarage in 1941, then returned to live there in August 1942.

**Herbert**, a German refugee, was arrested as an Enemy Alien in 1940 and interned in Canada. Upon his return to England, he lived at the Vicarage for two months from October 1941, then left to join the Pioneers. In May 1943 he enlisted with an elite company of paratroopers. He wrote often to Molly and visited when on leave.

**George**, an Austrian, was also interned in Canada. He was at the Vicarage from December 1941 to April 1943 and worked in munitions before joining the RAF in July 1943. He spent a long leave that December with the family.

## NEAR NEIGHBOURS

**Bert** and **Winnie Ackroyd** lived at 20 Duke's Avenue. He was a church sidesman. Of their five children, **Joan** is mentioned in the published letters.

**Robert** and **Ada May Austin** lived at Lingard House in the Mall. He was a War Artist and she was a writer. Their three children were **Rob, Peach** and **Rachel**.

**Baroness Bonnor** was Annie Susan Eliza Bonnor-Moris, 23rd Feudal Baroness of Main, also known as Nancy. She lived in the Mall at Homefield House.

**Harry** and **Rose Annie Bonnett** lived in Pages Yard, Church Street. He was a verger and she occasionally cleaned at the Vicarage.

**Bill Bryant** of 27 Park Road was an air-raid warden.

**Mrs Chandler** spent some nights in the Vicarage cellar during air raids.

**Mrs Craig** ran the post office at 15 Church Street.

**Mr** and **Mrs J F Croasdell** lived at Thamescote, a house in the Mall. He was an engineer. There were two grown daughters, one named **Anne**.

The **Drews** were a young couple mentioned by Molly in 1941. The wife's name was **Peggy**.

**Dr A W M Ellis** lived at Bedford House in the Mall. After he left in January 1941, he agreed to let Molly plant vegetables in his front garden.

**Ralph** and **Marjorie Edwards** were at Suffolk House in the Mall. He was Keeper of Woodwork at the Victoria & Albert Museum and first chairman of the Old Chiswick Protection Society. Their three sons were David, Timothy and Nicholas. It is worth noting that the middle son, Tim, a member of Lawrence Rich's 'big boys' gang', was the prime suspect when the Vicarage outside loo was blown up with a firework.

**Stewart Elmslie** arrived early in 1942 to replace Fred Wright as Edward's curate. He lived at Red Lion House in the Mall.

**Walter** and **Lottie Elwell** lived at Belle Vue, in the Mall. He was a churchwarden and Head Brewer at the local Griffin Brewery (now Fullers). Its cellars sheltered many residents during air raids. **Amy**, one of their two daughters, is briefly mentioned in 1940.

**Fred Farrow** did odd jobs at the Vicarage and often fire-watched with Molly at night. In her letters, Molly always used his surname to avoid confusion with Fred Wright, her husband's curate.

**Flossie Garnett** was originally at 18 St Mary's Grove. Miss Garnett is not mentioned in the letters, but merits an illustration on page 16 because Molly was so fond of her. She was bombed out in September 1940.

**Sir Percy Harris** lived at Morton House in the Mall. He was deputy leader of the Liberal Party.

**Margaret Hay** lived in Kensington but the family came to church at St Nicholas. In March 1944 they were bombed out and moved to Chiswick. Their children were **Robin** and **Heather**.

**Neville** and **Cecily Heaton** lived at The Hollies (now Heron House) in the Mall. They arrived at the end of 1942 with their son **Nicky**. Soon after, Cecily gave birth to another child. Molly became great friends with the family. Neville Heaton's team of officials headed R A Butler's education reform which was among the most successful statues ever. It remained the foundation of education policy for 44 years.

**A P Herbert** of 12 Hammersmith Terrace was an author and MP. There were four children, **Crystal, Jocelyn, Lavender** and **John**.

**Commander Blois Johnson,** RNR, was based in London at the Admiralty.

**Miss Joseph** had a flat at Island House in the Mall and volunteered with Molly.

**Drs Tom** and **Mary Nelson** lived at Eynham House in the Mall with their daughter, **Elizabeth**, known as **Bett**.

**Thomas Owen** lived at 1 Belle Vue Cottages in the Mall. He was an air-raid warden. Of the family's three children, **Peggy** is mentioned.

**Dr** and **Mrs R K Porteous** lived at 67 Chiswick High Road. He was the family doctor.

**Wilson** and **Jeannie Rae-Scott** lived at Longmeadow in the Mall. They had two children, **Philip** and **Midge**.

**Mrs Aletta Saunders** lived at Red Lion House in the Mall until February 1942. Of her three children, **Peter** is mentioned.

**Miss Shaw**, a lady of intellect, had a flat at Island House in the Mall.

The **Sisters of St Denys** were Anglican sisters living at at St Denys Cottage on Church Street. They assisted Edward with parish work. The electoral roll of 1939 lists two names, **Louisa Mary Weymouth Marsden** and **Alethe Stone**.

**Gerald** and **Anstace Spencer Pryce** lived in Pages Yard, Church Street. He was an artist of the First World War. After their house was bombed in September 1940, they left London.

**Mrs Stevens** lived nearby and would sometimes sleep in the Vicarage cellar during raids. She had two sons.

**Bert** and **Una Townsend** lived at 6 Chiswick Square. Bert was a churchwarden. Their son **John** was in the RAF.

**Nicolas** and **Peggy Volkov** lived at Latimer House in Church Street. He was an engineer and she was an editor. There were three children, Sophie and twins Marthe and Caroline and a cook named **Tata.**

## MOLLY'S FAMILY IN HERTFORDSHIRE

**Helen Richardson**, Molly's widowed mother, had a house near Ware called Amwell Bury. Patience and Anthea stayed with their grandmother during the school term early in the war and Molly and all the children would often visit during holidays.

**Mary Richardson**, Molly's sister-in-law, lived nearby at Rookery House with her daughter, **Moona**, aged 3.

**Major Ralph Richardson**, Molly's brother and the husband of Mary, served in the Army in Kenya and other parts of Africa.

**Captain Richard Richardson**, called Dick, was Molly's youngest brother. He served with the Seaforth Highlanders in Ethiopia.

**Richard P Croft** (Lt Col, British Army, retired), Molly's Uncle Dick, lived at Amwell Bury and was in charge of the Home Guard of Ware. His former batman, **Panther**, kept the Colonel's kennel of 40 Cairn terriers in the old stables at Amwell Bury.

## MOLLY'S FAMILY ELSEWHERE

Molly's two married sisters, **Avril** and **Nancy**, lived in Kenya (then Kenya Colony).

Molly also corresponded regularly with Edward's family, including his parents in the United States and a sister in Trinidad.

*Miss Flossie Garnett, a parishioner and great friend of the family, informed Molly that the Vicarage was full of ghosts. This was indeed true. Edward led the family in procession all through the house, sprinkling the rooms with water and saying appropriate prayers.*

*Edward and Molly with Helen and Patience, en route to a wedding where Edward would officiate.*

# ABOUT OTTO

Otto was born in March 1919 in Vienna, four months after the armistice of the First World War. Though the fighting had ended, Austria's troubles continued, with inflation, unemployment and increasing anti-Semitism, particularly after Hitler annexed Austria in March 1938.

Life was impossible for anyone of Jewish heritage. Over 350,000 Jews eventually left the region and 50,000 found refuge in Britain. Otto's older sister Myra moved to England in the summer of 1938 and worked as a housemaid near London. In Vienna that November, Otto was among hundreds of young men rounded up for two weeks' imprisonment. Upon release he left his law studies and managed to get to London in January 1939, but could not find suitable work or lodging. By March he was already deeply unhappy when he heard of his mother's death. He was thankful to find a home at the Vicarage in April, referred to the Rich family by The Society of Friends relief agency. He trained in printing, studied English and Spanish and helped Molly in the house and garden.

Otto's security did not last long. When Britain declared war on Germany in September 1939, all German and Austrian nationals in Britain were registered as Enemy Aliens and classified from 'A', for known Nazi sympathisers, to 'C', for those perceived as no threat. The following May, as Hitler overran Europe and made plans to invade England, the British government ordered the internment of many Aliens in all categories and arranged to send over 10,000 of these men and women to the Dominions.

Otto was arrested on June 26, 1940, fourteen months after joining the Vicarage and sent to the Kempton Park Racecourse in Surrey, which had been converted into an internment camp. He was then transferred to Huyton Camp, a former council estate near Liverpool. It was a month before he could write to an increasingly anxious Molly, whose reply became the first of over 600 letters that followed him throughout the war, first to internment camps in England and Australia and then, after his release and enlistment, to the camps of the Pioneer Corps and Army posts in England, France and Germany.

Among Otto's many devastating wartime experiences was the sea journey to Australia aboard the HMT *Dunera*. The grossly overcrowded ship transported 2,800 German, Austrian and Italian internees on a two-month voyage in conditions so appalling that three of the ship's escort officers were court-martialled. Winston Churchill later called the treatment of Enemy Aliens "a deplorable and regrettable mistake", but there has never been an official explanation of why so many refugees, some of them prominent artists and scientists, were considered dangerous enough for deportation. Official records are sealed until 2040. There are first-hand accounts in *The Dunera Scandal: Deported by Mistake*, published in 1983 by the Australian journalist Cyril Pearl.

When Molly wrote her first letter on July 23, 1940, the Rich family had yet to experience the rationing, the record-cold winters and the terrifying air raids of the Blitz. Otto had not yet embarked on the brutal two-month voyage aboard a prison ship to Australia. None of them knew that they would all face six years of war.

It was a year and a half after his arrest before Molly and Otto would meet again.

*Anthea and Patience dancing with the Sisters of the parish in their tiny, spotless kitchen.*

# 1940

*Alice lived in a room off the kitchen. When in spiritual doubt (which was often), she would pluck a tiny rolled-up Bible text with a pair of tweezers from a hat she kept in her wardrobe. Having read the message out loud and clear, she would emerge full of renewed fervour.*

**One month after his arrest as an Enemy Alien, Otto is allowed to write to Molly from an internment camp at Huyton, near Liverpool. This is Molly's reply.**

Dearest Otto,

Your letter has just arrived – I do not think I have ever been so thankful to see a letter before. For a month now we have had bishops looking for you and London is littered with letters and postcards begging people to go to camps and enquire for you. I have sprouted an enormous tuft of white hair on either side of my face and am covered with wrinkles. You will not recognise me when you come out. Do you remember I had nightmares that I had lost you? Well, they all came to life.

I am so glad you have found kind people in Huyton Camp. How interesting to meet a sculptor. I always think artists are so much more satisfactory than musicians. They have more mental poise and are more dependable.

I knew the food would be bad. During the last war, I remember red worms in the fish at even my most expensive school. Tent life is pretty awful, but half the male population of England is sleeping under canvas or in horrid little huts and again it is nothing to the discomfort of the trenches in the last war. One bit of your letter was scratched out. Did you or the censor do it?

I am sending you heaps of soap. I'm told it's difficult to get in the camps. Myra[1] and I are both sending you books.

I do not know what I am to do about the garden now you are gone, or about so many of the other things that I want you to do so badly and have not time for myself now Alice[2] is gone and I am doing the cooking.

The Belgian refugees are still here and we had a scene with them the other night. There is dancing on the green at Chiswick Park

---

1   Myra, Otto's sister, worked as a housemaid at Mill Hill, a neighbourhood then on the outskirts of London.
2   Alice, Molly's impossible domestic, left the Vicarage in 1940.

every Saturday evening and all the Belgians from round about go. The children get pennies and cakes and the grown-ups have a good time. However daughter Denese went out in the dark with a strange young man and Madame, her mother, was so angry she forgot to be unhappy. Now they both go out in the evening and take baby Albert, which seems hard as he returns so sleepy he can hardly keep his eyes open. Madame and Denese have both been much brighter ever since.

With love from MR

**Molly learns that Otto has left Huyton Camp.**

JULY 27, CHISWICK

My dearest Otto,

I saw someone who had been to Huyton on the 24th and looked out for you especially, but was told you were not there. I cannot think why they would have moved you yet again without any notification.

The Belgians have left for a few weeks so I can close the house during the holidays if I want. I'm not sure they will return in the autumn, which is just as well because the babies, though sweet, spend the whole time making noises like parrots just to annoy Madame. I think it would drive Uncle Edward dippy to have them back. The babies need smacking, but it is no good saying that.

Now that they are gone, we are thinking of taking in lodgers to help fill up the house[3]. I want two boys, big or little, failing these, girls. Fred [Edward's curate] says I shall get bedridden old ladies, which is really more likely. I thought I should like boys because I miss Lawrence and you so much. I have put myself down officially as being the mother of two boys and three girls[4], so whatever happens there will always be your room ready for you when you come back.

---

3   In 1940, the living of St Nicholas was £960, roughly £42,000 today. The wartime tax rate rose from 29 per cent to 50 per cent, while the cost of living increased dramatically as well. Molly had a small private income, but money at the Vicarage was always in short supply.

4   Molly's children were Helen (12), Lawrence (10), Patience (8) and Anthea (6). All were away at school. Molly considered Otto her fifth child.

Helen came home today and Lawrence yesterday for the holidays. It is nice to hear people in the house again. It has been so quiet with the Belgian babies gone that I wanted to stand in the middle passage and shout and make a noise. My children are bigger than ever and Lawrence is getting all pulled-out looking with growing so much.

With love from MR


**Molly receives word that Otto is at sea, en route to an internment camp in Australia. She now writes from Amwell Bury, her mother's house in Hertfordshire, where she spends the end of the summer holiday with the children.**


AUGUST 4, AMWELL BURY

My dearest Otto,

After endless enquiries we have been given a Melbourne address for you, though we still have had no official information that you have left England. I will ask the Mothers' Union representative for Melbourne to look out for you.

We have just heard that Dick[5], my little brother serving in Ethiopia, is wounded and missing and probably a prisoner of war. I am waiting to see what the third blow will be. The English have taken you away and the Italians my brother. I suppose the Germans will do the rest.

We are with my mother for the holidays. The weather is lovely, with the woods all dappled and shining and the ferns green and gold like lace and the sky clear and blue. And it is all passing unnoticed because people are too unhappy or worried to bother about it.

My other brother, Ralph[6], is home on leave and Mary and Moona [his wife and daughter] are here at Amwell Bury. I am glad we were all with Mother when she got the wire about Dick. The first wire said he had been killed and then another came updating the first.

---

5    Molly's brother Richard Richardson was a captain in the Seaforth Highlanders.
6    Molly's brother Ralph Richardson was an Army major.

I wonder if you will be allowed to write when you arrive in Australia. Tell us what the country is like. I will write both airmail and ordinary mail once a week, though right now I cannot think of anything to say. Life has come to a blank, like one of those novels by Thomas Hardy. Uncle Edward is reading them and says they are quite awful and steep one in gloom.

With love from MR

My dearest Otto,

Mary has produced a very old and simply enormously tall bicycle and I go shopping on it. It is just like riding a giraffe and one has to leap in the air to dismount. The little country towns are full of ladies riding high bicycles very slowly instead of driving cars and quite a lot of charming pony traps have been dug out of barns and outbuildings. They are so quiet and peaceful, it seems a shame that it needs a war to bring them into use again. When we were children we had a pony trap until my sister drove us up a bank and tipped our governess out and broke her arm. After that we took to a car.

I hear one of the great things about Australia is the space. I suppose it is like America, where distance does not seem to count and people do not bother to put fences round their gardens. You will not be overcrowded in camp as you were in England, that is one thing to be thankful for.

Mrs Austin lost her job as a censor. Her boy Rob got mumps and she had to stay at home to look after him. I am sorry because they needed the money. Robert[7], her husband, is working for the government. He is a wonderful artist, his finished work is so lovely it takes my breath away. The beauty lies in the composition and the line and detail. I cannot think how he will use that gentleness and tenderness in war work.

With love from MR

---

7   Robert Sargent Austin, RE, RWS, RA, was a noted War Artist, engraver and print-maker and also illustrated books written by his wife, Ada May Harrison. In the early 1960s he designed the only ten-shilling note and the first pound note to feature a portrait of Queen Elizabeth II.

*Amwell Bury, where Molly's mother lived until the house was
converted to a holiday home for bombed-out women in 1941.*

My dearest Otto,

A friend says letters from Australia are taking a month to arrive. I know we shall not hear from you for a long time and we do so want to know what has happened. I wrote to Red Cross headquarters and they answered almost at once. They will see you get clothes. I am sure it is very hot and you have not anything suitable. They will find out where you are interned and see that you are not put in with a lot of Nazis.

Moona, my small niece aged three, left a tap running in the bathroom and there was nearly a flood of one wing of the house. We all had to take off our shoes and stockings and bail the water up.

Did I tell you my Uncle Dick now keeps 40 Cairn terriers here in the old stables? Most of them belong to people who want them looked after temporarily. They used to attack Bonzo [the family Dachshund], but he now takes the offensive and can manage them all single-handed. Lawrence has been having a lovely time with Panther, the kennel man, learning how to shoot rats with a catapult. Panther is rather remarkable. He is in his third war and taking an active part, this time with the Home Guard. He was my uncle's batman in the Boer Wars and wounded in the Great War. He has a dead leg but can hop about very swiftly. He takes the Cairns out into the woods every day and speaks to them like people.

We are all well and the weather is lovely still. No more news about my brother. It takes so long to hear of anyone these days. I have got your little clock going and it gains nine minutes per week instead of ten per day. The regulator is pushed as far as it will go so I cannot get it quite right.

With love from MR

*Panther took the Cairns out into the woods*
*every day and would speak to them like people.*

My dearest Otto,

The new bureau for giving information about internees does not seem capable of answering letters, so I am going up to interview them on Tuesday.

Patience is supposed to have weak eyes and the oculist has to put in belladonna ointment before he can test them. They have been done for three days now and the poor little thing has enormous eyes with entirely black centres. They look odd in her tiny white face and she cannot see very much.

The children have all been swimming a lot at Haileybury[8] and Lawrence can now do a width and a half of the baths. I have been making clothes, also doing hours of housework as mother's maids have been having bits of holiday. I made Patience and Anthea overalls – long trousers like workmen wear. They look so sweet, I wish I could send you a snapshot.

There is loads of fruit everywhere, but we need rain to swell the plums and apples. We planned a picnic at a lake the other day, but when we got there the water was dried up.

Bonzo caught a rat and killed it. Perhaps it would be more correct to say a rat (an ill one) ran into his mouth and got itself between his teeth. Anyway he has one rat to his account.

There is a wonderful oak tree here that has been struck by lightning in the field, split right down the middle from root to top branch. Some of the oaks in the park must have been babies when William I landed.

My sister wired from Kenya with the news that some of Dick's native regiment saw an Italian officer take him away. We think he is the only prisoner, so he will not go to a camp. It is so awful that both you and Dick should disappear into the night and be impossible to trace.

Love from MR

---

8    Haileybury College was near Amwell Bury. Its swimming pool was freezing cold and
     due to be closed, but Helen Richardson persuaded the school to keep it open.

*Anthea and Lawrence with Bonzo and his brother.*

My dearest Otto,

They are making changes in the internment policy here because of the outcry from everyone who has anything to do with refugees. Cheer up dear, I think perhaps things may end up for you better than seemed possible.

It is not what they call 'very quiet' at the moment. We are made mad by my dog and Mary's dog quarrelling, also by aeroplanes, which are as noisy as the dogs. The other day we all watched from the lawn a great battle above our heads, our Spitfires against their Messerschmitts, with airmen parachuting down from burning planes[9].

I shall be glad to be going home tomorrow, it is difficult sitting about with nothing to do.

> With love from MR

My dearest Otto,

We are back at the Vicarage. I hope these letters will find you. Miss Coverley [a neighbour] says no letters ever get to her sister in Australia and airmail are as bad as the others. If anything really important happens we will send you a cable, but it is very expensive. In about six weeks' time all sorts of people will start sending you things and I hope by then we will know where you are. At least neither you nor my brother Dick will be cold next winter, not like the people who are prisoners in Germany. Cold does add to misery very much.

Did I tell you about Madeleine Carroll[10]? When France gave in she was reported missing. Apparently she had an orphanage over there and went to see the children and got cut off by troops. In the end she escaped by aeroplane.

---

9     RAF pilots defended the airfields of England from German air attack in the Battle of Britain all through the summer of 1940.

10    English actress Madeleine Carroll was best known for Alfred Hitchcock's *The 39 Steps*. Active in nursing and relief work throughout the war, she was decorated by both the French and US governments.

Gracie Fields[11] has fallen from popular favour because she and her new husband went to America and Government officials let them take large sums of money out of the country, while the rest of us, as you know, are not allowed to take more than a few pounds. I do not think she will ever come back again.

Alice went to look after a family in the Mall but soon left for a nursing home, where she was to feed the invalids. The first day she had a violent quarrel with one of the patients and left that evening. She is now in the country.

Everyone is sleepy from two nights up and sitting about fire-watching without anything exciting happening anywhere near[12]. I guess we will have to get used to it. Mrs Stevens [a neighbour)] had one of her children home the other day and let him join an ARP [Air Raid Precautions] practice for fun. He was to take the place of a casualty and be lowered by rope down the side of a house. They bungled the thing somehow and dropped the poor child, who landed on a brick and hurt his back. He is better now.

With love from MR

AUGUST 29, CHISWICK

My dearest Otto,

Yesterday I went to the new bureau set up by the Home Office at St. Stephen's House near Westminster Bridge. Of course they knew nothing about lost internees. There were several other people with me, foreign women in tears and Englishwomen in frightful tempers. I then went on to Australia House, up lifts and down marble passages and past a lot of haughty and beautiful blondes, till I came to a little man with round glasses like an owl. He gave

---

11    Entertainer Gracie Fields left for California because her Italian husband would otherwise have been interned. Parliament raised a question about the cash she took with her, then cabled an apology after learning it was officially earmarked to encourage US support of the war effort.

12    There were a few night-time raids in late August and Londoners 'fire-watched' to ensure that incendiary bombs were quickly located and extinguished. The sustained attacks of the London Blitz would begin ten days later.

me an address at Melbourne Barracks to write to for your camp number.

I am finding it difficult to get my mind fixed on Australia. My relations are scattered in all parts of the world except Australia, so I have never taken any interest in the place. Now I have a son out there.

Love from us all, MR

AUGUST 30, CHISWICK

Dear Otto,

Tell us what you can see from your hut or tent and what the other people in your new camp are like. I hope you will learn to play chess. I am trying to find out what you are allowed in the way of books and papers. Do you get news of England? We are all right and have heaps to eat and plenty of time doing nothing.

Helen nearly blew the house up the other day. Someone had been shaving in the bathroom when I turned out the gas at the main. Then later Uncle Edward turned it on again and the unlit gas beneath the shaving water filled the room. Enter Helen, smells gas, produces matchbox and is just stopped in time from finishing all our troubles.

You said I would soon get fed up with cooking, but I have pleasure in informing you that I love it. It is much more fun in wartime when you cannot have everything you want and have to think things out. I suppose everything is more interesting when a bit difficult, like writing poetry rather than prose.

My mother gave us a black Manx kitten to deal with th e mice. It is settling in and walks with  its back legs slightly apart, like a tiny hyena with no tail.

Everything is very tiresome at the moment. Everyone, everywhere, is away. I do not understand it as they must be in England and certainly the war must be somewhere. It is dull and dry and hot. The garden is like a brick and even the apple trees have died. The cabbages were so eaten by caterpillars that Fred Farrow, the odd-job man, had to burn them all. We are eating the second crop of peas. I wish so much that you were here all the same.

Did I tell you that the Government had to ask the Americans to stop sending food to England? They explained we were well fed and that the parcels took up too much space in the boats. There was also a rumour in America that a plane containing Goering[13] had been shot down and the body taken to London to be identified. The rumour was afterwards contradicted. It was not Goering, but a barrage balloon that had been shot down by mistake.

The Ackroyds are still going strong. We met Joan[14] the other day, who informed us in one breath that she had a marvellous new coat, a heavenly air-raid shelter and a perfectly divine hat. It was refreshing to meet someone so pleased with everything.

With love from MR

SEPTEMBER 3, CHISWICK

My dearest Otto,

I have written again to the Home Office and filled in another form. And I have written a fierce letter to *The Times*. If they print it I will cut it out and when you are an old man you will be able to read it to your grandchildren.

There is such a lot I should like to tell you but cannot. Although it is not 'news', it might come under that heading and not pass the censors.

There are crowds of refugees bathing in the river. They have brought soap and towels. The water is particularly filthy just now owing to the drought. Crickets are flourishing. Their singing reminds me of beautiful, peaceful places like Pennsylvania and Uganda. The other night while fire-watching at 2 am on the Mall I saw cats and heard an owl, a cricket, rabbits (in hutches) and chickens (in coops) and Fred Farrow had an enormous caterpillar crawling up his leg. We felt as if we were in a jungle.

With love from MR

---

13  Reichsmarschall Hermann Goering was Commander-in-Chief of the Luftwaffe.
14  Joan was the eldest of the five children of Bert Ackroyd, a church sidesman. They were a warm and friendly family. Bert found the bicycle that Molly relied on so much for shopping.

My dearest Otto,

Do you remember 'Jack the Gardener', who lives in a barge up the river? She appeared yesterday looking odder than ever in a most extraordinary pair of shorts. She had to move her barge and during the journey (she borrowed a tug to tow it) it fell to pieces and now she has no roof over her head. I almost offered her a bed here, but refrained from doing so as I thought Teddy would hate it. She is trying to buy another barge.

Baroness Bonner [a neighbour] has started a canteen. The whole thing is very Bonnerish, just filthy. Everything gets put on the floor: cloths for drying up, cups and spoons and tea and teapot lid. The floor is too dirty for words. I found a drying-up cloth the other day that was black, so I soaked and washed it and got it fairly clean and felt I had performed a good piece of National Service.

There are so many seagulls on the river these days. They woke me up this morning, they screamed so. I think they have been driven in from the coast. They do not understand what is happening.

With love from MR

The London Blitz begins September 7 at 5.30 pm, when 340 German bombers arrive with an escort of 600 fighter planes on a raid that lasts thirty minutes. Two hours later, guided by the flames below, more bombers hit those same areas over the course of several hours. On this first night, Chiswick receives a few incendiaries that do little damage. However there are soon fatalities, on the nights of September 16th, 17th and 21st. The Blitz continues for eight months until May 11, 1941, with over 70 major attacks on London and thousands of smaller strikes. In September, Molly takes in two couples evacuated from London's East End, which is hardest hit by the raids: Mr and Mrs Adams, their daughter and son-in-law, the Morleys and their dog Micky.

My dearest Otto,

I understand you have arrived in Australia. We do not often get a post now, but each time it does come I get so excited thinking there may be something from you. Of course there never is, as your letter, whenever you can send it, will take at least a month to reach us.

One of the most wonderful things about this war is the milkman. The post may be held up and the eggs not arrive and all sorts of things disappear from the shops, but the milk always comes. I have seen the milk lorry rushing down the road at 2 am braving raids and gunfire.

We have wired the Victoria Barracks to find out where you are. One can send a cable reply paid at 7d[15] per word, paying the same per word for the person who wires to reply. You have to guess how many words will be needed at the other end. Just now I think Australia is a good thing on the whole. The unselfish part of me is glad you are not here. Europe, Asia, Africa and N. America have all been or soon will be messed up.

We have just met Mr Elwell[16] taking the grandchild out for a walk in its pram. He looked rather like a barrage balloon and inside the pram was a little baby balloon. Quite a sweet balloon and remarkably like grandfather.

My evacuees are all having baths. They needed a certain amount of pushing towards the bathroom, but I had more success with them than you had with the Belgians and in the end they went. They said, "What happens if we are all lathered and the siren goes?" Old Mr Adams actually was all lathered when the siren went, but he took it very calmly, finished his bath quietly and came downstairs. He is a dear old man and a night watchman. The son-in-law works in a big scent and face-powder factory and the daughter has got a job at the Standard Yeast factory, which is nice and near at hand anyway, just behind the Vicarage. Oddly enough old Adams really ought to

---

15    7d is the equivalent of £1.30 today.
16    Walter Elwell was a churchwarden and Head Brewer at the nearby Griffin Brewery (now Fullers). There has been a brewery on the site since the 17th century.

spell his name 'Adames', it is a French name and his ancestors came over as refugees at the time of the French Revolution. I should think they were probably a good family because his face is just like the pictures you see of French people of that date, a long nose with a wobbly end and pale blue rather flat-set eyes.

I wonder if you will ever get any of these silly letters. After the war I shall have to come out to Australia and find you. I shall work my way as a stewardess. I think I should be good with seasick people. We have had no news of my brother Dick, either. My uncle has asked the Duke of Alba[17] to get in touch with the Roman Catholic Bishop who looks after the Romans out there. We think we may get some news through the Church via neutral Spain.

With love from MR

SEPTEMBER 23, CHISWICK

My dearest Otto,

We took Helen and Lawrence back to school on Thursday. We had Bonzo with us and in the excitement of finding Helen her new dormitory he got upstairs and ran right into one of the Sisters, who was rather annoyed. At Lawrence's school one of the Headmasters also has a Dax [Dachshund], a great hulking black and tan, so he got on very well there.

I heard from the Home Office at last. They are economising and write on funny squiggly bits of paper and use scratched-out envelopes. It is quite heartening to find such economy in high places. Anyway they said you were no affair of theirs and told me to get in touch with the Australian Commissioner in London, so I shall go to Australia House again tomorrow. I think one can get more out of an interview if one can see people and everyone at Australia House has been most awfully kind to a troublesome woman who asks tiresome questions they do not know the answer to.

This house is in a wonderful state of cleanness now. Mrs Adams polishes the hall so highly that it is a work of art to cross it and not

---

17   Jacobo Fitz-James Stuart, 17th Duke of Alba, was Ambassador to Britain for the Spanish National Government.

to slither down. The front and back doorsteps are blazing white and shine up so brightly in the blackout that I am afraid an enemy plane might take them for signals. Even the old copper behind the back door, which no one has looked at for the last 50 years, is white. Mr Adams is an expert at stoves and lights the one in the kitchen with ease.

I met 'Jack the Gardener' again yesterday. She was wheeling a wireless set as large as herself on a bicycle. She asked after you. She has not been able to find another barge so now lives in a room. It does not sound as romantic, but I am sure her barge was horribly unsanitary. We somehow got into a half-hearted argument about ancient buildings. I said it would be too awful if anything happened to St Paul's and she said it would not matter because there were heaps of people only waiting for a chance to build things just as lovely and buildings did not matter, only people. I have now got into a muddle about it all, because although in theory I should be horrified if St Paul's disappeared in the night, it would not have the stunning, hellish terror for me that the disappearance of you and Dick have had. I think this is one of those questions that have to be considered in cold blood when there is no chance of its ever happening.

Mrs Saunders [a neighbour] has let her upstairs flat at Red Lion House to a young couple who are exactly like each other. They might

*Jack the Gardener.*

be twins – they look as if they have been turned out by a machine with no emotions. Anyway they pay Mrs Saunders rent and without them she could not have stayed there.

We got another letter from my sister in Kenya last week. The news about Dick seems more vague than ever. In a way I wish she had not written, because it has just upset my mother again.

They have started water buses in London[18]. They go from Westminster down the river. I want to go in one some time. A P Herbert[19] has been trying to get them for a long time. I hear London used to have them, but they were too expensive to run. It will be interesting to see if they can keep them up now.

Four swans have just flown up the river. They look so lovely and white with their necks stretched out and their great wings flapping slowly. There are black swans in Australia – I have seen them in the zoo.

I wish I knew where you are. The Government of Australia will not tell us. I do not know why, as there is not anything we could do about it even if we wanted to. Somehow I would feel better if I could look you up on a map.

With love from MR

SEPTEMBER 27, CHISWICK

My dearest Otto,

I went for a tour round London yesterday in quest of information about Australian camps. First I went to the Red Cross in St James's Palace. The rooms are all lovely and one wanders down passages or through red brick courts and meets very smart people with titles and jewellery. They promised to do what they could. Then I walked across the park to St Stephen's House and filled in the form one

---

18  London River Services commandeered pleasure cruisers to replace train services dis-
    rupted by the Blitz, but the scheme soon proved too expensive.
19  Alan Patrick Herbert lived nearby at 12 Hammersmith Terrace, where a blue plaque
    from English Heritage describes him as an "Author, Humourist and reformist MP".
    Knighted in 1945, he served in the Royal Navy Division in the First World War and
    loved the Thames all his life.

always has given one – I can do it without looking now – and had a fierce conversation with the man in charge. I was feeling rather odd after having been up fire-watching the night before. I'd had exactly 1 hr 20 mins' sleep. After that I popped into a lost property railway office and got an umbrella as it was raining. The man in charge was keen on my buying a fur coat instead, but I do not like the idea of second-hand furs and anyway I hadn't the money. I got a red umbrella and it cost very little less than new. Then I bought a cake and a carton of milk for lunch and could not find anywhere to eat it but a damp bench on the Embankment.

The editor of *The Times* refused to print my letter because he said conditions were so much improved in the camps. It was a very good letter.

We all have bad colds, otherwise we are well. Myra will have written with her good news – she is going in for training in chemistry. I am so awfully glad and think it is the first nice thing that has happened to her since she came to England.

The Adamses and the Morleys have dug themselves in. Madame, Denese and the babies came round today to see if they could come back, but the rooms are not suitable now. No one will live at the top of a house because of the bombs. I like them and am sorry. Do you remember Mrs Volkov[20], across the road at Latimer House? She has three Belgian mothers and their three babies arriving next month. I gave her all my cots and sheets.

Love from MR

SEPTEMBER 28, CHISWICK

My dearest Otto,

We have at last found out your address from the Victoria Barracks. I also went again to Australia House and saw a Colonel Wheeler, who seemed quite human. Amongst other things, he said internees would have plenty of books and papers to read. Now that I know

---

20   Dr Peggy Volkov was editor of *New Era of Home and School* and worked from home after her offices were bombed.

you see the papers I shall not have to be so careful what I write and can tell you how we are getting on. I am really very glad you are out of all this. It is nasty having people flying up in the air above one's head all night long throwing bits of exploding metal down onto one with the intent to kill. You see there is nothing the civilian can do except rush off to a dugout underground. This is so awful that many of us risk staying in our own homes.

Last night all the part where Miss Coverley lives was wrecked by a landmine. She and two other older women are all homeless. Miss Coverley's niece, Gem, is a nurse and her hospital was bombed twice. The second time she had to sit with a dying man all through the bombardment. I think it was wrong to risk the life of a nurse by keeping her with someone who had to die anyway.

You will have read in the papers about the wonderful way in which a man took that great bomb away from just outside St Paul's Cathedral. Unexploded bombs are such a bother. Streets are roped off and the people who live round are turned out of their houses because these wretched things are expected to go off at any minute. We had Hogarth Lane out of bounds with one for a long time. They also dropped a bomb on the laundry and although it did not do much damage, the lame man who collects the washing fled in fear and we have had no clean things ever since.

Incendiary bombs are a bother, too. We had about 20 about a mile away on The Groves the other night, mostly small ones that people could put out themselves, but they had the fire brigade for two houses. This old Vicarage is wonderful. It rocks in the blast of the guns and the bombs and the windows rattle and shake. It sounds like a ship in a gale, but because it rocks and shakes, it is more safe than the tight, compact modern buildings.

The air-raid shelter at the Griffin Brewery is crowded every night. I think the people really enjoy it. One night Mr Austin went in and started sketching it all. At first no one noticed him, then they began "Look, he is sketching us! I won't 'av 'im drawing me, see he's drawing you now – look at 'is eyes!" In the end they got very angry and attacked him and he only just got out in time. I told him I should very much object to being sketched when trying to sleep in a shelter at night, looking too awful and not having been warned what was going to happen.

Mrs Volkov has gone away for a few days, leaving me in charge of her Belgians. One is having a baby at any moment and if it arrives in an air raid (and they all do), I shall have to ring up hospitals and doctors and things and get her off.

We have a French officer who comes to the shelter every night with his wife. He stands bolt upright in amongst all the sleeping people, in full battle dress, including his helmet. The Hollies has been taken by Dutch people and last night there was almost a riot because the old men outside the shelter looked up at the windows of The Hollies and said, "There's a Dutchman signalling to the enemy". They got the Frenchman to go out and translate as they told the Dutchman he would be murdered if he did it again. They seemed to think all foreigners speak the same language. The Dutchman said he had no blackout in his house and had turned on the light to find his coat. The people from the shelter said, "Why did you switch the light three times and how was it that every time you switched the light a bomb dropped"? I did not hear the end of the story as I went back to bed. I sleep on a camp bed in the study, with Uncle Edward on a divan. Fred Wright and Tasher the spaniel still sleep in their room upstairs. The evacuee couples go to the brewery each night.

Baroness Bonner made a lot of money on her canteen, then tried to make too much and now the stuff she sells is so bad no one will buy it. She and Mrs Saunders had a good old row about it and for two terrible days they tried to run it together. Mrs Chandler [a neighbour] is now helping. Actually she does most of the work and the Baroness messes about in the background.

I am so thankful to know where you are and want to hear from you very badly. If you only arrived September 6th we shall have to wait some time. You are missing nothing here. The raids have stopped for the time being and we are all getting on with the war. Cheer up dear, it cannot be for long.

With love from MR

My dearest Otto,

You very nearly did not get this letter, as your adopted mother nearly went. A mass of exploding iron whizzed over my head as I sat in the Post[21]. It was so near we could not hear it, just the bang as it landed about ten yards off.

We have a lot of young evacuees in the brewery shelter just now and they come over to me in the mornings to wash. Mrs Adams is very good with them and helps a lot.

Miss Coverley is coming to live with us now that she is bombed-out. I am giving her the little girls' room overlooking the river as a sitting room and the little blue room as a bedroom. Of course we only use rooms as clothes dumps, as it is still too dangerous to sleep upstairs. I have got to unfurnish two or three rooms as Miss Coverley will bring all the furniture she can squeeze in. I am rather worried because she has a few valuable things that have been in the family for generations, which she must leave in the old house. I fear they will be ruined with damp, but they are too big to bring here. I wish you were here to help and do not quite know what I am to do about it. Mrs Morley would have helped me, but she has sprained her arm stuffing yeast into sacks and cannot do much. Her husband is away all day and the others are too frail.

By the way, Hogarth House[22] has been hit and none of us has ever seen it. It just shows one should do things at once, as the chance may go if you do not.

I have been down to Hammersmith Town Hall lately helping the WVS[23]. We were collecting clothes to give to people who had been bombed out of houses and had nothing left. All sorts of people come to be fitted out. Anyone who has been bombed can get a paper

---

21   'The Post' was Air Raid Warden's Post #31 in Mawson Lane.
22   The house belonging to 18th-century artist William Hogarth was preserved as a museum. Severely damaged in the raid, it did not reopen until 1951.
23   The Women's Voluntary Service was founded in 1938 as a civilian defence organisation. Its one million wartime members ran rest centres and clothing depots for bombed-out civilians, staffed canteens, volunteered in hospitals and darned socks for the Army – 38,000 pairs per week.

from the Town Hall with an order for clothes. Most of our people are very poor, but occasionally we get quite well-off people who have just lost everything. One family came to be completely fitted out twice, they were bombed out about a month ago and again three days ago.

We also send clothes to the various rest shelters where people go if there is a delayed action bomb in their street. Everyone has to turn out of their houses for one of these time-bombs and they may be at a rest shelter for days till the bomb explodes of its own accord or is removed and exploded somewhere where it will do no damage. The Bishop of Kensington and his wife spent a day in a rest shelter because of a time-bomb in their garden.

We also give clothes to people who are being evacuated. When they are living at home they do with very few clothes. For instance hardly any of the poorer folk ever wear nightgowns. They seem to go to bed in their underclothes. They cannot afford to plonk down a couple of pounds for thick shoes, underclothes and woollies for the countryside, so we give them what we can. In London we are getting fewer and fewer children coming for things, because they are all evacuating. Lately we have had nearly all men coming for things to wear.

*Miss Coverley, a bombed-out parishioner, moved into the Vicarage with her cat and canary in September 1940. The children found her rather bossy and prim, but Molly was devoted to her.*

A lot of the clothes were sent from America. The way old clothes are sent across the world is really odd. First we send ours to Turkey, then to Finland and now America is sending clothes here. It would have been better if we had all kept our own and saved valuable shipping space. The clothes sent from America are not old, they are very good actually, but completely different from the garments worn by our people. I do not imagine the evacuees will even know how to get into some of them. It will be the story of the shorts sent by the English to the non-short-wearing Spaniards all over again.

We have no gas and no light at the moment and now cook on the dining-room fire by the light of a candle. One can get quite a lot on an open fire. Thank goodness we still have water, though they told us yesterday it was to be cut off. As we have people from the schools over here to wash in the mornings we need rather a lot. One bomb aimed at the church fell among the soft rubble where they have been pulling down the houses of Fisherman's Walk. It did no harm, only broke a few windows, but no one minds about windows any longer. We have all ours, so have the Elwells, but most houses have lost theirs and seem to get on all right without any.

I think we make an unnecessary fuss about those sort of things. Very few of us have undressed to go to bed for about a month now, but we sleep just as well in our clothes. We have also discovered that although it is nice to lie down to sleep it is not necessary. If one is tired enough one can sleep very well bolt upright on a small hard chair.

The people I am sorry for are the ones who are frightened. Lots of them are. It is so odd, all my life I have been afraid of things, but this does not frighten me in the least, as the children are away. Some people say they enjoyed the last war and now I know why. It is exciting and takes away from the humdrumness of life and I have never minded death. The Air Raid Warden's Post as a whole are frightened, but Fred Farrow and I quite enjoy it all.

I have written to see about correspondence courses for you at the camp or you will be speaking awful German-English with an Australian accent next time I see you.

With love from MR

*Miss Coverley and Molly prepared
dinner on an open fire by candlelight
when the gas and electricity were cut
off by bombs.*

My dearest Otto,

I am so tired I cannot type this letter. I hope you can read it. We had mild excitement last night when I heard a noise like fireworks and realised it was incendiary bombs. One fell on our corner but Fred Farrow and I put it out. Another fell on those old buildings by the river that are locked. Mr Volkov appeared with a stirrup pump all coiled round him and we rang up the fire brigade and tried to beat down the big doors. In the end the thing burnt itself out. One unexploded bomb was picked up in the churchyard, a lovely silver thing about a foot long. This morning Mr Bonnett[24] came rushing in about 7 am, too delighted for words, to say something had fallen in the Parish Hall. He has dropped 50 years and become ten again.

Helen has had a raid near her school. She seemed to enjoy it but had no water for days after. We have our light back, thank goodness. Someone has just written to say she heard Chiswick was 'destroyed'. It just shows what people will say. I wrote back to tell her it was anything but destroyed.

I spent the morning getting the two rooms ready for Miss Coverley while Fred Farrow turned out the cellar, which was full of awful junk, some of it 50 years old. Mrs Bonnett is making us a super shelter there, but I do not intend to sleep anywhere but the study. This afternoon I spent in the WVS. Most of the helpers were rather cross, as we all have our own ideas how these things should be done. Tonight I am at the Post again.

It is so disappointing about Myra's chemistry course. As she does not live in central London she would have to pay three times as much for her lectures. I do not know anyone she could stay with in London proper now.

I wish we could hear from you.

With love from MR

---

24    Mr Bonnett was a verger and his wife cleaned at the Vicarage.

My dearest Otto,

I have a feeling that you will not receive my last letter as I put in all sorts of things I should not have said. Anyway we are all well, well fed and things have been very quiet lately.

Gem came here yesterday to see Miss Coverley settled in and arrived speechless, she has lost her voice completely. The matron of her hospital is very much to blame for not looking after the young nurses properly. She slept for 16 hours on arrival. Miss Coverley has brought her cat and canary. I hope we will not have to keep running after the cat and bringing it back, it is bound to return to its old haunts.

I have sent some money to your Commandant in the hope that he will be able to cash the cheque. I know you will want all sorts of little things like shaving brushes and toothpaste. Also I should be happy if you had a few shillings for a cable if you changed your address.

I am so thankful that Alice has finally left. I do not think I could have coped with her just now. She wrote the other day from Reading to get me to buy an Aga cooker, saying it would save on our big gas bill and things boiling over. She does not realise that the gas bill was so large *because* she always boiled things over. Now that Mrs Adams and I are doing the cooking, the bills are normal, though we have no gas at all now after the last raid.

Anstace Spencer Pryse[25] will come for a few days to get her things out of their house in Church Street, which was bombed. They are very lucky – all their furniture is intact, with china cups still hanging on the dresser where they left them months ago. I found one of their lavender bushes out in the road and another inside the house, on a bed in an upstairs room.

With love from MR

---

25 Anstace Spencer Pryse was the wife of Gerald Spencer Pryse, an artist of the First World War. After their house was bombed, they stayed at the Vicarage while salvaging belongings for removal to a family estate in Wales.

My dearest Otto,

I went up to the Red Cross on Monday and they are going to try to get your release. They have been so good and helpful. Next war, when I have not so many evacuees, refugees and internees to look after, I shall give large sums to the Red Cross. I have bothered the Home Office a lot about you already. They will just mutter "Blow that tiresome woman, there she is again" and shelve my letter.

Micky, the Morley's dog, is rather naughty now because I have been taking him for a walk at 10 before going to bed, so he whines from the time the Morleys leave for the brewery shelter till I take him out. It is one of the reasons we are creating a shelter here. The cellar has been cleaned out, whitewashed and 'shored up' by Fred Farrow, that is to say props of wood have been put in from the ground to the ceiling to make it stronger. I have moved in four beds to turn it into a nice room for both couples. It remains to be seen if Mrs Adams will go there at night.

We had rather an exciting time the other day, but I am so tired I cannot tell you about it now. I have not slept properly for ages because of the fire-watching and feel all wuzzy. When I type, the letters come in the wrong order.

I met Madame the other day. I hardly recognised her as she had had a bath and washed her hair. She was quite a different colour, two shades lighter and so much brighter. Her hair is real carrots, not auburn.

We went to see Anthea and Patience last week. They are very well indeed and steadily getting worse and worse at lessons. It is annoying to marry a clever man and then have all your children take after their mother. Anyway it cannot be helped and perhaps it is as well they came as three girls and one boy instead of two of each as I wanted. After this war, character will be needed more than brains and all the children have lots of that. We can only hope it will be the sort required.

The Elwell's daughter Amy is doing Miss Coverley's blackout windows for her, like you did for the dining room, only the stuff we get now comes from Woolworths and is glued, so one only has to lick it and it sticks like a stamp.

With love from MR

**On the night of October 8, bombs land on Church Wharf and ignite barges full of wax destined for the nearby Mansion Polish works. Molten wax flows into the Thames, creating twenty-foot flames on the water. Strong winds and intense heat threaten St Nicholas and all the houses of Church Street evacuate.**

*On the night of the great fire on Church Wharf, Tata brought out her icon and prayed to St Nicholas.*

My dearest Otto,

We had quite a lot of excitement here the other night when some buildings caught fire and it looked as if this house and the church and all our block would catch alight, too. We looked out in the evening and saw the sky red with fire and great pieces of burning wood like huge glowing stars blowing everywhere in the sky. Flames like clutching arms were coming over the church and house. Uncle Edward said "Only a miracle can save the church now" and we all rushed out to salvage what we could and to see that the other people in the street turned out of their houses.

Most of them were in shelters where of course they did not know what was going on above them. Uncle Edward and Fred Wright and some other men took all the valuables they could from the church and Miss Coverley and I made up bundles of clothes and put things like the bicycle and the typewriter and some sheets in the garden. We took the three dogs, (Bonzo, Micky and Tasher on one string and fighting) and the cats and the canary, out of the house. The cats got away and were lost and some of my shoes slipped from the bundle under my arm. We gave the dogs to someone who lived near the Warden's Post to look after. I put my clothes tumble-down by some little bushes and we returned to find out what was happening. By this time the fire hoses were all the way down our street like great fat worms. Some were full of holes and soused us as we passed and Fred stepped right into an open hydrant. Later I found the cats sitting quietly by the kitchen door staring at the blaze, so I rolled Miss Coverley's cat into a sheet and picked up little Dinah (our kitten) and took them to the Post, where Mrs Stevens kindly said we could put them in her house. On our way home we suddenly heard wzzzzzz over our heads and lay in the gutter to let the little fellow pass. We had to do this three times and it seems a pity there was no one about to see us, we must have looked so comic. I was dressed in my best coat with the fur collar, as that seemed the best way to salvage it and a tin hat. Miss Coverley was in a tin hat and trousers. Well, when we returned, everything was vivid red with firelight and we did not have to bother about blackout for the first time for over a year.

Tata, the Volkov's Russian cook, saved the situation by bringing out her icon and praying to St Nicholas and suddenly the wind changed and blew the flames where they could do no harm.

By this time the alarm had gone round that the Riches and their house had gone up in flames and it was rather interesting to see how the neighbours reacted. The Townsends took out their car and motored straight off to the other side of London without waiting to see what had really happened. Some nearby families stayed in their houses and hoped in a very worried way that we were all right and the Rae-Scotts[26] came rushing down to see if they could do anything. So did Denese when she heard the same rumour next day.

In the morning we had to bring back the animals and of course we did not know who had taken the dogs, as we had handed them over the fence by the light of the fire and so we had to go around asking for them. Mrs Stevens returned the kitten, who had screamed so much during the night that her neighbour thought she had a nest of kittens instead of only one. Fred Wright found one of my shoes and I found another under a bush and my other best coat landed in the Elwell's shelter. I lost nothing but a few hours' sleep. Fred went over the garden for me with his lamp and we brought in the typewriter and bicycle before the rain started.

We are still waiting for the baby of the Volkov's Belgian to arrive. The telephone over there is out of order and Mrs Volkov and Miss Bigg [her secretary] have come here to do their ringing up. The night of the fire the Nelsons[27] had a lovely time giving tea to the firemen. They rushed out with steaming cups on trays. I wish you had met the Nelsons. They are awfully nice and frightfully funny. He is completely circular, like an enormous egg, with square glasses and the mentality of a clever boy of 18. She wears slacks and looks exactly like a stout penguin and is much more clever than he is. They are both doctors at hospitals – he is a heart specialist and she works with women and children in the East End.

---

26  Wilson and Jeannie Rae-Scott and their two children, Philip and Midge, were good friends of the Rich family.

27  Drs Tom and Mary Nelson were family friends.

We are having such lovely autumn weather of sun and mist and coloured leaves. You never saw any proper weather in England because all the time you were with us it was cold and wet.

With love from MR

My dearest Otto,

Both Spencer Pryses are here and we have had a hectic time with them as they are from the wilds of the country and know nothing of our London ways. We were to dine with the Nelsons and Anstace tried to go with a revolver tied round her waist. In the end we persuaded her to leave it behind.

We got back about 10.30. They did not like the idea of sleeping in the cellar with four strangers and I was afraid they might insist on sharing my sofa and Uncle Edward's divan in the study. However I was very firm and got them downstairs. Then Mrs Chandler came in (she was also sleeping in our cellar that night) and I discovered the Spencer Pryses trying to undress in the cellar surrounded by sleeping people. In the end we got them undressed upstairs and then brought them down to bed and they quite enjoyed it.

Just as we were starting off this morning Gem walked in and announced "I have come", apparently for the night. I was terribly busy getting the Spencer Pryses off and cooking meals for Fred Wright and getting beds made up in the cellar and so put her in charge of Fred's meals. By the way, that blackout you did for the dining-room window was a great success. One half is perfectly all right and if you had not done it we would have had trouble with all of it.

With love from MR

My dearest Otto,

I wish we could find out how many letters you receive and how long they take to reach you, but there is no way of discovering this.

The Red Cross think there is a good chance of obtaining your release and the question now is, what will you do? Will you stay in Australia and get work or return as a Pioneer[28]? Probably everyone in camp has been discussing these questions and you will know more than we do about it.

We are still having an exhausting time with the Spencer Pryses. They keep going up to London and getting caught in an air raid so they cannot get back again. They leave us their gas masks and other useful things but still cling to the revolver. They were caught again last night and returned this morning in a taxi with 20 parcels. We persuaded them to leave some of the parcels behind to be picked up with their furniture next week, but they still left looking like Christmas had come to stay. Their family estate in the country was given to their ancestors by Edward III and its 150 farms pay their rent 'in kind', that is, in goods instead of money, so there is no rationing there. They brought us some lovely butter and meat. There is an old avenue of trees up to the house and they say the removals van will not be able to get through, so they are going to have the trees lopped. I hope they will check with the family.

With love from MR

OCTOBER 28, CHISWICK

My dearest Otto,

We have seen the Spencer Pryses off at last. They were trying to persuade the removals men to let them travel in the furniture van, apparently so as not to have to pay the railway ticket home. It was my fault, because they would not have thought of it if I had not suggested it. They left one of his pictures. It is a blodge of red and mauve and is supposed to represent an African flower.

With love from MR

---

28 Initially only British citizens could serve in fighting units. Foreign nationals were assigned to the Pioneer Corps, an auxiliary labour force that built roads, field fortifications and military camps.

My dearest Otto,

I hear arrangements are being made so that internees in Australia may register for the Pioneers out there and then return to England. You will find everyone here rather changed, I think. They have all got rather thin, which is odd because there is heaps to eat. Also their noses are inclined to be red and their faces white. I remember in the last war everyone got to look like that.

Lawrence stuck his hand through a glass window and cut a nasty gash in his arm. So silly, but something that every small boy has to do once in his life. Helen's school is not allowed baths because the summer was so dry the wells did not fill properly and there is not enough water.

We have had a very gay and un-warlike break for a few hours. Mrs Volkov, Miss Bigg and Miss Shaw, who lives at Island House, came to lunch. I do not think I have ever seen three women so much on the same lines. Miss Shaw went out to Nineveh[29] before the war and did drawings for the expedition digging up the remains of the old city. The result of having such really clever people in the Mall is that we are beginning to get together and to discuss things.

The Belgians came the other day with the children. Madame left her old pram and took the newer one back with her, promising that Denese would come and fetch the old pram next day. I said I would house it till then, but found it so dirty I could not allow it indoors.

Alice has just come in. She has returned from Reading, goodness knows why and is staying with her sister. She hopes to get another job in London.

There are a lot of young swans on the river. Their feathers are quite brown and will not turn white for another year. They are rather sweet.

With love from MR

---

29    Nineveh is located in what is now Iraq.

My dearest Otto,

We are rather worried because we have had no letters from you. I will send a reply-paid cable to your Commandant. If you are not at the address I have, we shall have to begin all over again to find out where you are, just as we did last time.

Things are so much quieter at night that I wondered if I should sleep in my room again and went upstairs to see how it looked. The ceiling was damp and clammy, the paper hanging in strips and we found several tiles had come off the roof. The really amazing thing is that there are any tiles left at all, what with all the bumps and bangs and bits of iron falling all over the place.

There are a good many very smart American ambulances about, grey with bands of red round them, each driven by a lovely lady dressed in grey to match the ambulance, with her lips done up in exactly the same red as the line on the car. All very smart and fetching, but I do not know if they have done any work yet.

With love from MR

NOVEMBER 22, CHISWICK

My dearest Otto,

There is very little news as nothing has happened lately. The raids have been over other parts of England instead of London. They do not tell us what towns are raided, which is rather a pity as everyone guesses and rumours fly around. It could not do any harm to let us know as the Germans must know themselves.

I am trying to get work at a mobile canteen. They rush about giving tea to the people clearing up London streets of debris. They tell us that we go out 'under fire', which sounds rather exciting, but as there has been no 'fire' lately to get out from under I suppose it will end up in being rather dull like everything else.

I have not had any answer to my cable about you. Perhaps cables are also censored and so take about a month. The Government promised to get the censoring done much quicker but they must have forgotten about it.

We went to supper at the Volkov's the other day and had a real Russian meal. First a famous Russian soup. We think it is called 'bosch' or 'bosh' although that sounds very odd and not very Russian. Anyway it was bright pink and full of little floating things and there was a dollop of butter in the centre. Then came chicken, which was boiled and cut up in exactly the same way as a rabbit. We were invited because of the chicken, as Mrs V had brought it back from the country. After that came a nice stewed fruit the same colour as the soup. Uncle Edward and Bonzo both felt very ill that night – I do not know why. The food seemed harmless and Bonzo did not have any as he was not even invited. People put boxes and baskets outside their doors at night and all the household scraps (i.e. anything that is not ashes or tea leaves or poison) are dumped there and collected by the dustman in the morning and taken away to feed pigs. Sometimes Bonzo gets in before the dustman. He yelped and cried and I had to rub his tummy and take him out at 5 am, much to my annoyance.

We had a lovely day today, all shiny and sunny, the river silver and splashed with misty bright colours. Tonight literally thousands of seagulls were flying inland, all in the same formation as planes, great spearheads all over the sky. When the birds come in like that people say there are storms at sea. We have had such wet weather lately and I have had all my clothes soaked in turn. I hope it will dry up a bit now.

Lawrence has managed to get ringworm at school. I cannot think how, as he has not been away from school for weeks and is the only boy who suffers from the horrid complaint. I may have him back earlier as he has to be isolated and it is so dull for him. There are a lot of skin diseases about. Gem has a ward of soldiers with various mild complaints of that sort. Those things always rush through a country in wartime. It will be nice to have Lawrence back again – it seems a long time since I saw him last.

With love from MR

My dearest Otto,

We were so glad to get your postcard at last; we were so worried about you. I want to know many things. What is the country like? Do you get lovely sunsets? Also what sort of language you talk with the other internees? What do you do?

Though we have had a quiet time lately, tonight the bombers are grunting their way across the sky again and we have had a couple of horrid whistles across our house. As neither of them went off with a bang they must be time bombs, or perhaps they fell in the soft river mud. Bombs in soft earth do not seem to do any harm, they do not even break windows. The nasty thing is to hear a whistle and then the scrunch of a building going down. Each plane carries eight or nine small bombs, so if one comes down you are quite likely to get the whole lot. Don't worry about Myra. If she is bombed out she can come here.

We have all become so used to noises at night that when there are no guns booming we find we cannot sleep. Lots of the poorer people do not like sleeping upstairs any more. When they are evacuated, they refuse to sleep on the top floor, preferring the kitchen or the parlour, which means the family on whom they are billeted have to live upstairs. Some insist on going to shelters to sleep even though there is no danger, because they like the company. Someone wrote to the papers that we were returning to being 'cavemen' and letting our 'herd instinct' run away with us.

We still have a lot to eat, but round things are going out of circulation, including eggs, apples, grapes and onions. I suppose it is their shape, they may be difficult to ship. The rations are ample. People who once used pounds of tea each week are far better for having less[30]. It has been proved that children were eating much too much sugar. Even the butter goes round all right and there are a great many fats not rationed. This letter seems to be about food.

With love from MR

---

30   The tea ration was 2 oz per person per week.

My dearest Otto,

We are going to Helen's confirmation tomorrow in Abingdon. On the way we shall stop at Oxford and see the Eldridges. Did you know them? They are a young couple. He worked in a bank and was an organist and she has gone blind and he is going blind. I do not know what has happened. Their eldest child is at school with Lawrence and they have no money. I would take in their youngest boy for a bit but should not want to give him back after a month or two. That is the worst of human relationships – you never know how much trouble you are letting yourself in for. It is selfish but quite true.

I told you I am bringing Lawrence home early because of ringworm. I have bought him a fold-up bed that will just fit in the space left over in the cellar. Mr Morley and Mr Adams will have to crawl over the sleeping forms of Mrs Stevens, Mrs Chandler and Lawrence when they want to go to sleep as Lawrence's bed will take up the little passageway left. I shall be so glad to have him back. There is no one young in this house now and I feel it should be full of young people. We are all so old, over 35.

I have another letter from Alice. I am afraid she wants to come back, but I cannot cope with her again.

I still have a pair of your shoes and your suitcase lying about in the room upstairs and when I go to get things from there it does not feel so much as if you won't ever come back.

With love MR

My dearest Otto,

Things have been very tiresome this week. It is awfully cold here and we have had quite hard frosts. I cannot get coke, so we have the boiler on just one day per week and we must all get into the same bath. As there are eight of us in the house, not counting guests and children, there is competition to be first. We got the little girls today (Mother brought them to Harrods to see the toys) and I discovered to my horror that Patience has developed the old complaint [nits]. So we have had to start with paraffin and vinegar all over again.

Harrods was looking very nice and the cracker room was lovely. It gave one a creepy feeling to remember that all those pretty, useless coloured things were made in Paris. I wonder if they will ever make them again. I hope not. They are just pretty and not beautiful and I hope in future we shall cut out prettiness and get on straight to beauty. After all the old Greeks did that and to a great extent the Romans of the first century and we should do so too. We all have a wonderful chance of starting fresh and making everything good when this is over.

Miss Coverley has been digging for victory very energetically in the garden. She wanted an allotment, but I put my foot down and said I refused to nurse her if she got ill. I promised to evacuate the garden entirely if that plot of ground would satisfy her. She has started hopefully, as we all do and I know she will be pleased till the beginning of July. After that the whole place dries up and becomes a desert and all the flowers die. I have told her this, just as the people who were here before us told me, but she does not believe it any more than I believed them.

Helen's confirmation was lovely. The chapel is white and there were 30 girls all in white and behind them the rest of the school in ordinary school clothes but all wearing veils instead of hats. The veils were different colours according to the house the child was in: blue (dark and light), green, yellow, red and pink. It looked lovely against the dead white all round and the sun came streaming in through the windows of plain glass. Outside it was blowing half a gale of icy wind and great Whitley bombers were roaring past. (Half a gale – nautical expression meaning a fairly stiff wind. Enough to make you seasick on a small boat but unnoticeable on a large one.)

The service was taken by a friend of Teddy's, the Bishop of Oxford. When it was over we took Helen out to tea and she bolted the most creamy cakes the shop could produce. (We are not allowed cream any more and it is pretend cream in cakes now.) We stayed in Abingdon for the night and then picked up Lawrence in Brackley. It was very difficult finding the way across country as there are no signposts left standing[31]. When we arrived we were in time for lunch, which we had with the boys. This was rather fun and they all talked and made much more noise than we were allowed in my day. Very good food, plain but nice. It must be difficult catering for a school in a war.

The school is in the line for planes coming from the Continent to the Midlands. The headmaster told us they had all the planes that raided Coventry last month. He said it was awful, one after another for hours. They heard them pass over, drop bombs, then turn back without a pause[32]. We started home directly after lunch with Lawrence and arrived here in time for tea. Very cold, sharp frost and we were glad to get home.

With love from MR

DECEMBER 16, CHISWICK

My dearest Otto,

Just a short letter to tell you we are all right. I will write again in a couple of days' time. Lawrence is home and we went for a walk on to the island[33] as the tide was out. At the end we found six dead swans. Mr Elwell says they were killed by a bomb, but I think they got their feathers covered with oil and died. In England we say that just once, before it dies, the swan can sing and if you happen to be about when a swan is dying you may hear the 'swan song'.

We went to see the Hamiltons[34] at Swan House the other day. He is rather a well-known poet. I happened to look at his hands. Do you remember telling me once that your fingers had stopped growing and were too short? Well his fingers are like that too. I do so wish you would try writing. I know you can. Perhaps you could write

---

31  Signposts from roads and even train stations were removed in anticipation of a German invasion.

32  More than 500 German planes bombarded Coventry over the course of 10 hours on November 14, 1940.

33  Chiswick Eyot is an island in the Thames across from the Vicarage; it can still be reached by foot at low tide.

34  George Rostrevor Hamilton was a poet of the First World War and also a civil servant. He was knighted in 1951.

poems, but they are not much use as people do not want them. They are fun to write all the same.

Things are very quiet and we have had no more bombs lately. Christmas is nearly here, but it does not seem like it. I wish we could skip Christmas Day for once.

With love from MR

DECEMBER 23, CHISWICK

My dearest Otto,

I have had Helen and Lawrence back from Amwell Bury for a few days. We had practically no raiding while they were here, except for the first night. Lawrence was delighted because he picked up a lot of shrapnel next morning.

We are in for a very long cold spell, I think. We have some coke in now, but it is the wrong sort and the stove has to be relit three times a day. However I get a bath this afternoon.

I wish a letter would come. We want to know what you are doing, even though news that is three months old is not very satisfactory. I read that one of the camps is going in for vegetable growing, wanting to become self-supporting. I hope you are at that camp because after this it will be a good thing for us all to be able to 'scratch a living from the soil'. We keep on hearing rumours about what is and what is not happening to internees. At first I believed them, but now I do not believe anything. That is much the safest plan.

We now have a couple of rabbits that are due to have babies soon, so I suppose this household will live on rabbits now, as we did during the last war. Lots of people are also keeping hens, even in towns. I should like some but Uncle Edward says they bring rats. The Volkovs keep them and they do well, though they get into the neighbour's garden and peck her cabbages. I am afraid it will be war between the two houses.

*continued next day*

I had to stop yesterday and cook the supper. We have Miss Osler coming for Christmas. Do you remember her? She is frightfully old

(60), rather sad and has nowhere else to go. I asked her to come for a few nights and sleep in our lovely cellar. She replied, "I do not mind where I sleep, I can roll up and sleep in the passage". I did not think that a good idea as the dogs and cats would walk over her at night, Fred would fall over her when he came in and Uncle Edward would run into her when shaving in the morning. In the end it was decided that if there is no air raid she will sleep in our one free upstairs room next to Fred.

I simply cannot think what to give the four evacuees for Christmas. Earlier I gave Mrs Adams 2 lbs of hoarded sugar because Mr Morley takes so much in his tea that she is always short. I am afraid she will have forgotten that and they do not seem to be in need of anything I can afford to buy them. I must stop now, as I have the children's dresses to alter and I have come to the end of my paper ration.

With love from MR

DECEMBER 29, AMWELL BURY

My dearest Otto,

I am here in the country with the children for half the week and at home for the rest of the time. It is difficult being in two places at once and needs a dual personality. We motored grandly down from London in a friend's car only to find that Lawrence had left his suitcase behind, so he's had only what he stands up in, which is already dirty. I got very fed up at first because I thought the case had been stolen.

The children had a good Christmas in London in spite of the war. Here in Amwell Bury, Lawrence has been rummaging in the attics and brought down a lot of my father's old uniforms. He goes to bed with a sword on each side of him 'to keep away ghosts'. It is funny for a modern child who does not mind bombs or guns and who knows all the planes by their sound, to be frightened of ghosts.

With love MR

*Molly's father, Major R M Richardson, 14th (King's) Hussars, served in India, Egypt, Sudan, and South Africa until 1903 and died in 1917.*

*Molly looking smart, carrying her gas mask and wearing her new turban hat.*

My dearest Otto,

This is New Year's Eve. There is one thing I know about the coming year: it cannot be any worse, however hard it tries, than the one that has just gone. They seem to have sent you to the best climate in Australia and I am grateful for that. So many poor wretches are spending this winter freezing in European camps.

I am afraid we will not get the letters you wrote when you first arrived because according to the papers some ships went down about that time. Our Christmas mail from the US has not turned up this year. You will have seen in the papers what happened in the City[35]. Do you remember any of those places or have they all got muddled up in your mind? The chief thing I remember about our expedition there is what a bad temper I was in when we started and how cold it was picnicking outside St Paul's.

We had a sherry party today. The chief topic of conversation was evacuees, as all the houses in the village have several strange children billeted on them. Most of the hostesses have become fond of the children and having them has turned a Christmas that might have been heart-breaking into something rather happy. I do not know what will happen when the evacuees return home. I am having Patience and Anthea back from my mother for a few days tomorrow. I shall be frightfully busy during their stay, but it is the only time I can fit in a visit before their school term begins.

Today the children went to a lunch and games party. We cannot have tea parties now because sugar, butter and margarine are rationed, but we can make paste and sardine sandwiches and serve tins of fruit and jelly.

There is no more room on the paper so must stop. This letter is so dull. I am sorry. I feel just dull and nothing else tonight.

With love from MR

---

35    The night of December 29 marked one of the worst raids of the Blitz, an attack that set fire to most of the City. St Paul's Cathedral miraculously survived.

*Lawrence slept with his grandfather's swords 'to keep away ghosts'.*

# 1941

*Molly used a newspaper to draw the
fire, once with disastrous consequences.*

Otto's camp in Australia is near Hay, an isolated town in the interior of New South Wales. His camp, one of two, houses 1000 men in 32 huts inside a triple ring of barbed wire with guard towers. After a 40-day mail embargo, Otto is allowed to receive mail and to post two letters per week, each limited to 150 words. Molly and Otto exchange letters that take three months to arrive, if the ship that carries them survives the journey. While Otto endures sandstorms, flies and heat, Molly and her family face record frost.

JANUARY 17, CHISWICK

My dearest Otto,

It is so cold I am sitting right by the fire with the typewriter on my knee. Some fish bought for Fred and Miss Coverley has just been discovered frozen to its dish in the larder, so we are thinking of starting a private refrigerator.

We have had little air-raid activity except for last night, which was surprising. I thought they would have frozen to their machines out there. One of the illustrated papers showed airmen in special electrically heated suits made of asbestos, I think. They looked more like divers, quite covered from top to toe.

I have two letters from you and know from them that you wrote five, so that gives an idea of how many letters get through. Do go on writing ordinary mail, as some people have a theory that they get through more regularly. Then repeat everything important in several letters, as we always do our end. Please let us know everything you can about your camp. It is not just for us, I will copy out what you say for the Austrian Centre. Tell us how many people there are per hut and if the people from one camp can meet the people from others, everything you can think of that would interest other people's relations.

With love from MR

My dearest Otto,

I was so glad to get your letter. I know you are unhappy, but no one with any imagination can be happy just now.

I am surprised that you got my letters about the raids – I thought they would be censored. No, I do not think it is brave of the English people not to mind being bombed, it is entirely a matter of temperament. English people love excitement of any sort, which is why we are either gamblers or very religious and we all read so many detective stories.

Uncle Edward and I attended a Church conference on 'how to put the world right' at Malvern College[36] with all sorts of interesting people, including Dorothy Sayers, a brilliant woman writer of detective stories. DS smokes endless cigarettes and the conference were all wondering what happened to the smoke as it never came out of her mouth, it just disappeared down her inside.

With love from MR

My dearest Otto,

It is cold and snowy. The snow is not the lovely, soft kind that comes down like fat and lazy silver feathers, but a small, hard, cruel snow that descends in tiny black balls from a black sky.

We went with Lawrence to see *Captain Blood* the other day. It was awful as there was no heating in the cinema and we felt like blocks of ice inside. Also the talkie arrangement suddenly stopped while the film went on. Errol Flynn went on talking with no noise coming out of his mouth and everyone in the cinema started whistling. The films these days seem to be so old. I suppose the Hollywood people will not trust their new films to the sea, or perhaps some of their best actors have gone and they cannot make many films now.

---

36   The Anglican conference was convened by William Temple, who was appointed Archbishop of Canterbury the following year.

We had a disaster here the other day. I left a newspaper in front of the dining-room fire to draw it. It caught alight, fell on the full wastepaper basket and set that alight and the whole thing caught the wall. I came in to find a blaze. I yelled fire and everyone rushed up with water. We hope to get the room entirely redecorated by the insurance.

We now have lady bus conductors. They have to pass stiff efficiency tests and medical exams. They are smartly dressed in grey with a little red to match the bus. They are an improvement on the men, I think. The trouble is that when these wars are over, you cannot get the girls out of the jobs and then there is not enough work to go round. It may be different this time as there will enough rebuilding all over Europe to keep any amount of people busy for years, if done properly. I think we shall all become masons.

I want to keep hens, but one cannot buy a henhouse and I cannot make one. I thought I might buy a cupboard and put perches in it but cannot find anything in the shops.

With love from MR

JANUARY 21, CHISWICK

My dearest Otto,

I have a new ribbon for the typewriter but must wait till Fred gets back to put it in for me. We have been to see Lawrence off to school and now the house is cold and silent. On Monday they are coming to repair the damage from the fire. We have shut up the drawing room and it will be rather horrid as I shall have no sitting room and no bedroom and in fact shall have to live in the hall. It is very wet and dark now, but at least it is getting lighter in the evenings. Before Christmas we had to put on lights as early as three o'clock.

We have been given sandbags to put round our houses in case of fires. Filling the bags is the difficulty, as the sand is heaped by the side of the road and if you are not very quick you find other people have swooped down and it is all gone.

We have started a fire-spotting organisation under Mr Owen[37]. We have a rota and if there is a raid the few people who are left along the Mall – and quite a few have left – take it in turns to do 3½ hours spotting for fire bombs (incendiaries). These are easy to deal with if found in time. One was put out by a lady of 99. We are three teams: ours, the Nelsons and the Owens, each with a stirrup pump and three able-bodied people to work the thing. There are so many empty houses it is really rather dangerous. By the time a team with a pump and a bucket of water have located the keys to a house and rushed about the place, losing their way down passages and battling to open trapdoors on roofs, the place could be well alight and the team with it. Anyway it will be rather fun and I hope I shall be the first spotter to see a bomb fall.

With love from MR

JANUARY 24, CHISWICK

My dearest Otto,

We have had some more bad news in the family. My brother-in-law was killed on an aircraft carrier[38] and has left my sister Nancy with three little children, including my godson. Also we are afraid there is now not much chance for my brother Dick.

I have bought two huge packets of peas and will get a man to dig up the lawn. It is such hard work. Last time I tried I nearly broke in half and was bad-tempered for a week. I hope to get the peas in rotation with carrots and onions. This soil is too light for onions, but it is horrid not having any.

We have had an awful time with mice in this house. I discovered one in the larder and drove it into that big box of cups and saucers. Then I shouted for the cats, but no one heard, so I took the box into the pantry, emptied all the cups out and found a lot of loathsome black beetles. When I came to the mouse, I tipped it and the beetles

---

37   Mr Owen was a local Air Raid Precautions (ARP) Warden.
38   Nancy's husband, John Wilfrid Harris, died January 10, 1941 in an attack upon the HMS *Illustrious*, which was escorting a convoy to Malta.

into the washing-up bowl, drowned them all and threw their corpses into the garden. Then I bought poison, put it on bits of bread about the place and seem to have killed off quite a lot of the creatures.

With love from MR

My dearest Otto,

I am glad you are where you are, although it is so far off. Distance does not make much difference nowadays. We can hear from you 10,000 miles away, but if you were only 200 miles away in Paris we could not get in touch with you at all.

The men are taking so long doing up the dining room I think it will be just about ready to be blown up by the next German attack. It will be pretty but a bit cold. I really like yellow or gold rooms, but they had no suitable yellow paper. There is not much choice these days. Personally I like a good all-over pattern, especially for a room that is used a lot, but they only seem to make plain papers now. Perhaps all the wallpaper artists have gone to camouflage government lorries and factory sites.

We have been having a few daylight raids lately, but no one minds them. They threw some bombs in the Chiswick baths, which fell on the sunbathing slopes. As there was neither sun nor sunbathers at the time it did not matter. A few bombs went in some allotments and dug up the winter greens, but even that might have been worse. It is, however, a bore if you want to go to a large shop. Each building has a 'spotter' on the roof and when the planes are overhead he blows a whistle, the shop closes its doors and the assistants go down to the shelters. If you are in a shop when the whistle sounds you are shut in, otherwise you are shut out. So you stand inside or outside and grumble or make jokes (according to your temperament) with the strangers round you. It is rather fun. Even the most sticky man or woman becomes quite human and interesting when the guns are popping.

With love from MR

My dearest Otto,

I had been away for a few days to see my mother and the little girls and on my return I found three letters from you on the hall table. One was written September last and explained so much we did not understand before. The second was written in October. This last letter arrived for my birthday, only two days late. It is lovely, because now all five of my children have written me birthday letters and until two years ago I had only four children.

When I got home I found the dining room finished and all the mess cleared up. It looks so nice with bright green paint and dull green walls. The curtains and carpet give it warmth and it looks like spring.

The new Bishop of London[39] was supposed to come here today, but they rang up to say he had a sore throat. It was very disappointing, a lot of people were coming here to meet him after church. He was to have stayed for lunch and I had been given an onion to put in a bean pie for him. It seems a waste of an onion these days not to have a bishop to eat it.

With love from MR

My dearest Otto,

It is so warm I am sitting writing without a fire. Teddy is away at the Lakes for a few days, Fred goes off next week and I had two days away last week, so we should be very fresh and full of beans.

I wrote to Myra asking her to consider getting trained at a really good hospital, but was too late. A letter from her crossed mine saying she plans to train as a machinist. I am sorry in a way, as a first-class nurse has been lost to the world.

We are now told we can get oranges for marmalade and I have saved some sugar. I will make some to eat at once and a few pots to keep till you come back, just for fun.

---

39   The new Bishop of London was Geoffrey Francis Fisher, Baron Fisher of Lambeth.

We have had no bombs for ages except one very suddenly in the morning a fortnight ago. It made a mess of a lot of buildings near here, but did not kill anyone.

We are planning a large meeting about the Federal Union[40]. I have asked Mrs Stevens, because she talks so much that telling her anything is as good as telling fifty people. The only way to forward international relationships at the moment is to get to know people, to learn to trust foreigners and get them to trust us. If the Bishop of London had come here last week I was going to ask him to arrange a meeting between our clergy and all the foreign pastors now in London. It must be done in some central place by someone with a bit of authority.

When I was a tiny girl I remember my mother talking about the people who never came back from the Boer Wars. When I was a schoolgirl I lost my best friends and all the people of my own age in the Great War. This war they took you. Next war, if there is one, I shall lose Lawrence. If I go on till I am 100, as you say I will, I shall have time to lose my grandchildren and great-grandchildren. Things cannot get any worse than they have been, so they simply must get better.

With love from MR

My dearest Otto,

Thank you for your letter that arrived yesterday dated Oct 20th. I think we get about one in five of the letters you send and you probably receive the same amount of ours. I shall write every five days so you should get two letters per month.

It is very cold and snowed last night, yet during the day the poor birds were singing, thinking spring had come. I have got a gas poker for lighting the kitchen stove. It is so difficult to light and sometimes we have to try six times before it will catch.

---

40   The Federal Union was founded in Britain 1938 and is now part of the World Federalist Union, which campaigns for world government as a means to end world wars.

They have pulled down all the end of Devonshire Road near this house and a lot of Hogarth Lane. It should have been done after the last war, as all the houses were condemned then. Old Hitler did with one bomb in one minute what we have been trying to do more gently for years. They should be able to build good new places on the old land. The trouble in Chiswick has always been lack of space for good working-class flats and allotments. Allotments are very necessary. Everyone likes making things grow and even if a man has been denied creative genius in other ways he can always get some of it out in a garden.

I have seen the newspaper reports about your voyage to Australia aboard the *Dunera*. I did not let Myra see it as the poor child has enough to cope with. As she reads a very low type of paper, she will find out soon enough.

Lawrence says a large part of his school is down with flu, including masters, which he thinks very satisfactory.

I am glad they let you bathe. What is the river like? Are there gum trees? Is the water warm?

There is a wretched pigeon in the garden here and as fast as Miss Coverley digs for victory to plant things, it scratches them up. Did you tell me once that you never notice the noises birds make? I think even you would hear our pigeons.

Uncle Edward asked Mr Austin if we could cultivate his garden now that he is away and promised we would put his apples in store for him. He, however, is full of old-fashioned feeling about private property and would not let us do it, in fact he was annoyed with poor Teddy for even suggesting it. So now we shall have to dig more of the lawn, which is a bore and backbreaking.

I am afraid this is a very dull letter. I cannot say any of the things I want to because of the censor.

Goodbye, with love from MR

My dearest Otto,

Dinah has completely disappeared. We think she must have been stolen. She was a darling, more like a dog than a cat and seemed to know what you said to her. Uncle Edward will miss her frightfully. My only hope is that whoever has her may bring her back when they find she is going to have kittens.

I have been to see Sir Percy Harris[41] about you. He lives in Morton House (the one with a horse on the door), which is small and perfectly lovely. Lady H is an artist with wonderful red hair. I told him you people in Australia were being forgotten and we wanted the Home Office to do something about it. He laughed mirthlessly (as they say in novels) and said the Government was inundated with letters about Australian internees. He learned how old you were and said "Oh, leave the boy where he is, you do not want to bring him back into all this". He may be right. He wrote to the Home Office and they said you had better volunteer for the Pioneers. If you come home as one you will remain interned until you are called up, but would get some leave right away. I have a feeling that everything is coming all right. All my bad feelings have come true, so I hope the good ones will come true, too. I think you will be back for Christmas.

I went into London to find out if Myra could train as a doctor. First I went to the nursing college in Queen's Square and interviewed the secretary and got the idea that everyone in the nursing world was longing for Myra to become a doctor. Then I went to Bloomsbury House and saw a Mrs W, a most alarming lady. I think she has been put there by the authorities especially to 'choke off' any wretched little refugee who might aspire to becoming a doctor. The gist of the interview was that Myra should be prepared to pay £100 per year and take five years' training. I made a very swift 'strategic retirement according to plan', as they say.

We are digging up the lawn as hard as we can. I try to do 6 ft per day. Not 6 ft square, but 6 ft long and 2 ft wide, like a grave.

---

41   Sir Percy Harris was Deputy Leader and Chief Whip of the Liberal party.

The Croasdell girls complain that their father has dug 'graves' all over their lawn. The Croasdells are a new family in the Mall at Thamescote. I am so glad they are here. The elder girl, Anne, is tall, about 6 ft, very clever and nice-looking. She has a club for Czech refugees in the City and helped get 30 people out before the arrival of Hitler. Mr Croasdell is an engineer and very Yorkshire. I think he puts on the accent because the rest of the family have none. You will like them – they know a lot of young people.

The Rae-Scotts from Longmeadow House were offered a whole sack of dog biscuits and refused them as they only have one dog and thought they would be landed with a lot over. Then they found they could get no biscuits themselves, nor could anyone else, so they have written to see if the offer still holds good. Bonzo has evidently been listening to and taking in, the wireless talks urging us to "eat potatoes for energy". He quite likes them now, although he cannot support the Government in its campaign to eat more carrots.

We have become so brave now that we sleep at the very top of the house and nothing could dislodge me again. If both Hitler and Mussolini crash a bomber on the roof I shall go on sleeping and take no notice.

All best birthday wishes, dear. I know this letter will arrive very late, but the wishes will keep.

With love from MR


FEBRUARY 28, CHISWICK

My dearest Otto,

Patience and Anthea are here for their half holiday and playing in the garden. They are very excited because a dead sheep has been washed up on our green by the high tide.

I have opened up another upstairs room because Gem is here and Myra comes to stay for a while on Tuesday[42]. She has finally left cleaning for that horrible family. Unfortunately the blankets have

---

42    Myra remained at the Vicarage until December.

run out and I am now reduced to using tights and fur coats and all sorts of funny things.

Dinah has turned up again. She had got shut into the room at the end of the top passage. Miss Coverley had to have her cat put to sleep. It was so old it could hardly walk. Mrs Saunders has also been having a bad time with cats. A pair broke into her house and made a nest. In the end she caught them and took them in our old baby basket up to Shepherd's Bush to a place where they kill cats. This letter so far seems to be all about dead animals.

I have put my name down for organising billeting in Chiswick. If there is a bad 'blitz' in any other part of London they will want me to force the inhabitants of this place to put up 2,000 people. It sounds so unlikely ever to happen that I agreed to do it.

We have all been to see *The Great Dictator*, the new Chaplin film. It is good, but nothing like as good as they said it was. Perhaps I have got so morbid about everything I cannot see anything funny, even about CC. Though it was amusing when he was in an aeroplane and the machine went upside down so when he pulled out his pocket watch the thing went straight up into the air instead of hanging down.

I hear Mr Wilkie is going to Australia[43]. He is a darling little man and we've missed him dreadfully since he left England earlier in the month. There was an update with each news bulletin. He always wore a tin hat, whatever was happening and he went about on buses and down to shelters and talked to old ladies who rushed up to give him onions. Everyone cheered him and shouted "We can take it" and he stood with tears in his eyes and replied, "Gee boys, I think you are great".

I am sorry this letter is so deadly. Perhaps there will be something more interesting to say next week. The little girls send their love.

With love from MR

---

43 Wendell Wilkie was an American politician. After losing the presidential election of 1940 to Roosevelt, he made a widely publicised trip as FDR's personal representative to Britain and the Middle East in 1941.

My dearest Otto,

We have had no letters from you for weeks. I dread they will just take you away again and leave us knowing nothing for months.

Myra is here, though not actually in the house at the moment as she went out at 7 am to look for work. It is difficult, but I hope just a matter of time. Everything is altering continually, with people being drafted into munitions and all sorts of people working who never did so before[44].

We had the Rae-Scott's daughter Midge in last night. She did not ring the bell in the usual way, but opened the door and called out "Is anyone here?" Of course Bonzo dashed at her and took a bite out of her leg. It was not a good beginning, but if you will bounce into people's houses without ringing bells you must expect their dogs to do something about it.

We had supper and then played the gramophone a bit and talked. Then there were voices in the hall and all the rest of the Rae-Scotts appeared. The house appeared to be full of them, although in actual fact they only numbered three. There seemed no way of getting rid of them. I was to be on from 12 midnight till 2 am fire-watching and Uncle Edward from 10 to midnight, so we all just sat and talked. Then they wanted to hear the Continental news at 11 pm, which they insisted was the best news of the day, but it sounded to me exactly like all other news. Halfway through a warning went. When this happens the wireless fades out and that made them leave at last.

I went down the Mall just after 12 and it was an absolutely perfect night. The moon was golden and almost full. In front of the Owens' house the tide was nearly up and 50 little ducks were busy eating in a very unrefined way, making a great noise. I thought it was odd there were no swans about, having seen so many in the afternoon. I then saw a great white hump at the end of the island.

---

44    Great Britain was the only Allied nation to conscript women, eventually requiring registration for those aged 19 to 50. Depending on their marital status and the age of their children, women were required either to serve in the auxiliary forces, to work in war industries, or to volunteer for service organisations such as the WVS.

It was the swans all together in a heap fast asleep. The ducks were small blobs of shadow on the still, grey-gold water and the island seemed like a cloud. I came across a fat and elderly man who had come out fire-watching by mistake on the wrong night. He found it all so beautiful he would not go back to bed. A few minutes later the 'all clear' went and we both returned home. Unfortunately there were two other warnings that night before my shift ended.

I am having a Mothers' Union meeting today. It is horribly cold and very wet and if the people coming are not frozen on the way here, Miss Joseph will speak to them. She is one of the many new people who have come to live here. She looks frightfully old and you would at once ask why she is not dead and buried, but she is very lively and always doing things. She travelled the world before the war and is now a fire-watcher and WVS member and constantly going out to lunch and tea because she gave out that she was lonely and all the people round here rushed up to make her feel at home. Her brother is a famous don at Oxford and she is frightfully clever, too. When very clever people get old it does not seem to matter so much. When merely intelligent people get old they become so slow and stupid. Personally I rather like old folk, especially old men. There is something restful about them.

*continued later*

*When Midge walked into the Vicarage unannounced, Bonzo bit her on the leg.*

Myra has returned and the long and short of it all is that she is going to train for a Government job, which is the best thing possible. We do not know where she will be sent, but before she is called up she will be able to stay on here. You would have been very proud of your sister the other night. I had left her in the dining room, which we now use as a sitting room, reading a paper. Suddenly there was a great bang and a bomb descended very noisily not far off. I rushed into the dining room and found her still reading, not having even looked up.

Gem arrived in time for supper and now the room is very noisy as she has the gramophone on and Myra is machining and I am typing this. It means shutting up part of your head so that you do not hear the rest of the noise.

With love from MR

MARCH 17, CHISWICK

My dearest Otto,

After a month of planning, our Federal Union meeting on Saturday was a great success. I gave two pints of milk and Mrs Croasdell gave some homemade cakes and the rest was given by Miss Shaw. Mrs Croasdell arrived with her husband, the latter trying to camouflage himself as some trimming on her coat, afraid he would be the only man. However there were quite a lot of them in the end. A young man with fair hair and a completely disappearing chin spoke to us at length (and very well) on the FU. It is a good idea and should be supported, though it will fail. The failure will be due to us, because we are not Christian enough to carry it through. Unfortunately the FU people do not see this. They think they can get on with their idea because it is a good one.

Miss Coverley and I must start planting seeds. We have been given a large chunk of the Elwells' lawn, which we share with Mrs Saunders. I got in two rows of peas and will add two more in a fortnight's time. I also planted perpetual spinach, which is terribly good for the blood. It goes on all the year round and the more you pick the more it comes. Mrs Saunders has been hard at work in slacks and long boots, her hair rolled up in a handkerchief, thoroughly enjoying herself. She has planted lettuce and put up dear little lean-to greenhouses with panes of glass supported by wire holders bought at Woolworths.

Mrs Saunders's friend in America sent her some special stockings. They look like silk but are really made of coal.[45] They do not ladder or do any of the unpleasant things that one's stockings usually do. They arrived done up in lovely cellophane paper and they are so 'sheer' one would have to do all sorts of things to one's legs before wearing them. It is practically like not wearing stockings at all.

I have given up afternoon tea for the war and find it a blessing not to be tied down to a meal at 4 in the afternoon. It also makes jam and butter go much further. Myra gazes in amazement at the amount of food we get through here but has not yet seen the helpings Mrs Adams gives to Mr Morley. He has only one proper meal per day and it cannot be good for him to put away so much at one time.

They have been very busy clearing up Chiswick lately and it all looks neat and tidy because we have had no trouble here for a long time. London is a different matter. Mrs Saunders's famous son had a narrow escape last week when asked by friends to go to a well-known dance hall near Piccadilly Circus. You will read all about this in your papers and by the time the news reaches Australia it will sound even more exciting than it did here in England. Peter could not go to the club as he had a cold and went to bed instead. His friends said as he was not going they would put it off for another day. The dance hall was bombed that night and a great many people hurt. Peter used to play in an orchestra and knows all the men in the band, the owner of the place and most of the employees. Mrs S was so thankful[46].

---

45   The 'special stockings' were made of nylon, a synthetic fibre created with chemicals distilled from coal. Originally developed as a silk substitute for parachutes, from 1940 it was also used for hosiery, called 'nylons'.

46   Peter Saunders was invited to the Café de Paris, billed as 'the safest club in London' because of its underground location. It received a direct hit on March 8, 1941 and more than 30 people were killed. Peter was a captain in Army Intelligence and after the war produced Agatha Christie's *The Mouse Trap*, which has run continuously in the West End since 1952.

All the people round here are becoming 'blood donors'. Midge went for a test with several girls from her office and only she and three others had the type of blood that is most needed. I should do this, but I hate blood so much it makes me ill to think about it.

I have been busy with the blackout because Mr Owen says ours is so bad we will be fined. The factory at the back of the house has spotters out during raids and one night they sent in to say we had lights flashing from a window. They said the light came from a part of the house that was not being used and we got in some wardens to see if they could find anything and of course they could not. It must have been moonlight on the glass, which has caused excitement with spotters before now. After that they were very cross and unreasonable. I have now got curtains that are nailed onto the kitchen windows and tied round the waist in the centre. They are not very pretty but will be effective. Myra has been helping me. She is also going to help me make a dress. It is dark blue with spots on it and when made up (I hope) it will be rather full in the skirt and have a sort of frill round the neck.

I must stop as there is nothing more to say. You must try to keep well and try to be happy. Lots of people ask after you and they all want to know how you are getting on. Do not forget that there are ever so many people wanting you to come back. God bless you dear.

With love from MR

MARCH 21, CHISWICK

My dearest Otto,

There is quite a lot to tell you about this week. We have had another blitz on the docks and it demolished the house where the Adamses used to live. Now that their house is permanently uninhabitable, they and the Morleys have taken a flat in Grantham Road. It is very nice, with a bay window and heaps of sun. They are leaving the Vicarage and they go in next week. I shall miss having them here and I do not know how poor old Mrs Adams will like being in her new house alone all day after having been surrounded by people. She may feel a bit lost.

Quite a lot of people are wandering back to Chiswick and today a whole line of Ackroyds appeared in church. We had a dear old visiting vicar to preach again last Sunday. He is very keen on the Americans and thinks their helping us means the beginning of a new age[47]. I hope he is right.

Miss Coverley is home again after a few days with her brother in the country. She and Myra get on very well together – it would be dreadful if they did not. If Myra can stay on at the Vicarage I shall give her a room of her own and an oil stove so she can get away from us all if she wants. I am so afraid she will be called up and have to go soon.

We are suddenly lucky with coke, coal and oil here and now have heaps. So many people are short of these things. Next winter we will all be living in one room just to keep ourselves warm, like a lot of dormice.

We had an amusing party at the Croasdells. They got a friend whose name appears to be just 'Edgar' to speak to us on architecture. He talked quite well but is very young and clearly did not think that anyone could know as much as he did. He showed us pictures of new blocks of flats, which he thought were lovely. We said we would feel like bees if made to live in them. He 'boosted' flats for another hour, then his sweet little wife gave the show away by telling everyone enthusiastically that they no longer lived in a flat, thank goodness, but had a house of their own.

One idea for our area is to build flats on ground formerly occupied by houses and allow an area for allotments. Edgar also discussed a big room attached to each block of flats where the children can play and the women can work, with classes for the men and Sunday services. He is right in that most of the troubles that arise in our existing flats in Chiswick come because there is no centre where the people can go. Now that the residents have been allowed to dig allotments, the grown-ups are occupied in the evenings. However children of all ages wander about getting up to all sorts of mischief.

---

47   President Roosevelt signed the Lend-Lease Act on March 11, 1941. The legislation allowed the US to support the Allied war effort with ships and planes while remaining neutral. America also supplied food, introducing powdered eggs and Spam to Great Britain. The US entered the war nine months later.

Afterwards we had coffee provided by the Croasdells and we all brought and 'pooled' sandwiches. There was no warning that night so no one had to hurry home and we remained out to the wildly late hour of 9.30. Next day we went into London to a lecture on Christian Education given by a Jesuit to a mixed audience. I am now feeling very highbrow, though all this talk does not really lead anywhere and is in fact a trifle disheartening. But if people do not talk they do not think and if they will not think they will do nothing.

After this improving remark I will tell you about the rest of the week. Chiswick Town Hall has given us all red forms asking our ages and telephone numbers so that we can become fire-spotters. As we have already been successfully fire-spotting for the past six months, we were rather annoyed. I filled in my form because Mr Owen brought it round and he has been so tiresome about our showing lights at night I thought it would help if I agreed without fuss. The people with perfect blackouts were in a better position and refused to be bothered. Actually I refused to fill in my age, but Mr Owen said most other people had objected too, so that was all right. There are very few of us down this end who can afford to tell our ages at Town Halls or anywhere else.

We are getting on with the vegetables. Directly I commence planting peas, all the birds in Chiswick come and watch, so I have put black cotton over them. We have some nice flowers on the table at the moment that were grown in the garden, they smell lovely and remind me of when I was a little girl.

We were very lucky last night and had no raid for our shift of spotting.

With love from MR


APRIL 9, CHISWICK

My dearest Otto,

Last night we had another bad blitz, during which I found a wonderful place from which to spot. It is under the balcony of Said House [in the Mall]. I took a stool and sat wrapped in a fur coat, with the house behind me, the balcony above and the wall on the left as protection from the blast. When the anti-aircraft guns went off, the house sort of shivered. There were some fires a long way off. You will have read all about it in the newspaper before you get this. Two nights ago we had a bad one as well, a noisy land mine. Miss Coverley and Myra and I came down and sat in the dining room, but Uncle Edward and Fred and Gem all slept through it. It was all so beautiful, the groups of falling flares, the gun flashes, the sudden glow of a fire leaping up to redden the sky and the ongoing glow of fires on the horizon. How can anything so stupid, brutal and cruel be so magnificent?

I wonder why you are not allowed to underline things in your letters. Would they think you are sending coded messages? Myra thinks the censor stopped some of hers because she grumbled so much. By the way, we are having a sweet little romance in the house just now: Myra and Fred. It makes me feel quite young and spring-like.

Milk is rationed, which is a bother as it makes things difficult for people like Fred and Uncle Edward, who drink a pint per day normally. They now only have three pints per week each.

Things just vanish from this house. Miss Coverley says she has lost half a dozen silver forks, but we think she must have put them in the bank. It would need a very hardy thief to come into this house full of people and dogs and creep up the stairs, which always creak and crawl about her room, where the canary cheeps if anyone enters and discover silver forks.

We are having sunshine at last and I am wearing cotton dresses again.

The peas we planted are coming up nicely. I have been busy making jam from rhubarb, as it is the only stuff we can get now. Even the apples are over. Myra brought me 2 lbs of sugar, so I had enough for Lawrence to take back to school, some for the children's holidays, some for ourselves and some for jam. Our ration of jam is only half a pound each month, so it does not go far. I shall keep some for your return. People try to give their sons jam to take back to camp now that soldiers' rations are the same as civilians', especially as Army cooks are not as good as we are at making food go round.

I am becoming a gastronomic expert and can almost make food out of air.

I went to the country with the children the other day. Mother had a party for them and it was lovely and sunny and the daffs were out. The afternoon was to raise money for a children's home and everyone had to bring their own tea. All the food was pooled and we all hated each other's. Unfortunately the party was divided, half nursery children and the rest older people. Nurse seized too much food for the babies, which left the other children short and Helen had nothing to eat.

Miss C's canary is fluttering about the room prior to having its bath in a soup plate. It is very sweet. There is constant war between the cat and the canary, with Dinah like a horrid German advancing with open mouth on a very tiny nation. We are all terribly proud of the Greeks. They actually are holding the Germans, which is more than anyone else has done so far.

With love from MR

APRIL 18, CHISWICK

My dearest Otto,

Myra is letting me have a couple of sheets of the air letter she is sending. It is a great responsibility to write a letter that costs 5/-[48] to send. We are so excited there now seems a real chance of getting you back and I have bought bales of wool to make you socks. Mrs Chandler and I arranged yesterday that those of us who had sons in the military could get the good wool they sell at the depot.

Lawrence returns on Tuesday, I am glad to say. The little girls are very well and we shall be seeing them tomorrow. Helen is flourishing.

Hogarth Lane and Avenue, the end of Devonshire Road and bits of Church Street have gone, so now the streets are ready for lovely new homes to replace the slums that Hitler has so kindly cleared for us. We are in no danger here now; things are very quiet and we have not seen such a thing as a bomb for ten days.

---

48   5 shillings would be worth £10 today.

We found a picture of my brother Dick in a paper, a photo of English prisoners in Addis Ababa. It was copied from an Italian picture paper. So we now know where he is and that he is well. We have not heard from him, partly because the town is so cut off from Europe and partly because he is probably not allowed to write.

They have turned Greenash [a house in the Mall] into a hostel for 'shocked' people and I am going there to help between 8 and 10 on Saturday and Sunday mornings. I made marmalade and have a 2 lb pot waiting for you. It is not at all runny and worth its weight in gold.

Do try and come back soon. We miss you just as much as when you first left.

With love from MR

APRIL 26, CHISWICK

My dearest Otto,

This will be an odd letter, as I am writing it with my left hand, having hurt my right one.

I am having another refugee soon, a German girl. We hope we will all get along. I assume Germans are much the same as other people underneath.

Gem arrived last week with a young man she met in hospital. He has been known to us for a long time as Silk Pyjamas because he wrote home to his people asking for some to wear instead of the cotton ones provided by the hospital. As that institution is full of people with nothing much to do (they are waiting for casualties which so far have not arrived), the pyjamas' arrival excited everyone very much.

Lawrence has scrubbed through two more pairs of trousers. I wish someone would invent iron clothing for small boys. It is awfully cold and we feel spring will never come. I wish you could send us a little of your heat.

With love from MR

My dearest Otto,

I went to see the exhibition of the London Group at Burlington House today. This is a group of young artists who annually send their pictures to the Academy and are annually rejected. Victor Pasmore[49] has his famous picture of cows. They are transparent and you can see the grass through their bodies. They are about the best thing in the exhibition. I also bought another umbrella at a railway lost-property place. They had hockey sticks and ice skates, so I might take the children in the holidays and fit them out.

Towards the end of the month I am going to see about cutting and replanting trees at Amwell Bury. Our woods are so bad, we really need a forester to advise about it all. Perhaps Lawrence will become one. A great many foresters will be needed after the war. All of Europe will need replanting.

With love from MR

My dearest Otto,

Our German refugee is called Ilse. She is a very young 18, very sweet and never reads the papers. She will go on thinking that her parents still wait for her in Holland. It is awful, as she will tell me about them and I cannot tell her what I know has happened there.

Gem is engaged to Silk Pyjamas and they are to announce it once he has got his commission, in three months' time. He escaped being sent abroad by one day because he was in hospital. She went to stay with his people and we had to buy her a new dress for the occasion and almost died of weariness and cold rushing from one shop to another to find something suitable she could afford. I insisted on going along because I knew the engagement would only come off

---

49    During the war, artist Victor Pasmore lived in the Mall at Riverside House and then at 16 Hammersmith Terrace.

if his mother took a fancy to her. He is only 22 and very fond of his mother. Miss Coverley looks years older after this excitement. She worries more about Gem than she would over her own daughter if she had one.

There has been so little rain that the garden will not grow and last night we had frost, very bad for the vegetables. My peas are said to be the best in Chiswick and have caused quite an excitement.

I have been given a bottle of onion flavouring. It is so strong it has to be kept inside a second bottle so as not to make everything smell.

We are having War Weapons Week[50] in Chiswick and my Uncle Henry[51] (to whom I wrote about you) is coming to open it tomorrow. I am selling War Bonds in an empty shop in the High Road on Monday. Tomorrow I am selling flags, as they forgot to get any sellers. It is a children's day and it seemed a shame that they should go without because some silly fool forgot them. I hate selling flags.

With love from MR

MAY 22, CHISWICK

My dearest Otto,

We still have had no rain. Nothing will grow, or if it does it is like leather. In an ordinary year it is a bother when we get no rain, this year it is tragic.

Dinah is supposed to be having kittens quite soon in the cupboard in Miss C's room. There is a heavy bet on about the date of their arrival and everyone is quite stupid over the cat. From the way they behave one would think no cat had ever produced kittens before.

Ilse is exactly like a lovely Persian kitten and says she was always called 'kitten' at home. She speaks English well, but with a Cockney

---

50  Each spring between 1941 and 1943, towns and cities throughout Great Britain hosted a week of special events to promote the sale of war bonds.

51  Molly's uncle was Henry Page Croft, 1st Baron Croft, a Conservative politician.

accent. On Friday she is going to attack the manager of the millinery where she works and demand higher wages. She could get war work and make much more, but it is a pity not to finish her training first. Hat-making has much more in it than you would think.

We have not heard for a long time from my brother Ralph, who is back in Africa. In his last letter he said he had been in a battle and that it was a curious experience. That was all. We can only guess where he is.

Peggy Owen is to be married. They cannot have the parish hall, it has been taken over as a rest centre and the other day a lorry delivered 100 beds and mattresses and stores of food. There are too many guests to squash into their own house, so they are coming here, which will be rather fun. We are giving them the ground floor. We will go to the wedding and afterwards shake hands and gently slide away. Mrs Owen and I are discussing cups and saucers and the possibility of eggs and marge for cakes.

Gem and I went on our bicycles into Kensington today and looked at a lot of expensive and lovely things before queuing for chocolate at Woolworths. It looked good but tasted stale. I think it was pre-war and they had found it tucked away somewhere. It is nice bicycling now as the roads are so clear. Gem paid 6d [£1 today] to see a tank on show for War Weapons Week, but the young man who showed her round was so shy he could hardly speak. Perhaps they put him on that job on purpose because they did not want people to know too much.

With love from MR

MAY 26, CHISWICK

My dearest Otto,

Peggy Owen and her young man were married on Saturday. Everyone gave the couple bits of sugar and slices of marge for the reception here and some people produced a few eggs. Between us all they had a wonderful spread. Somehow it was almost too much, because everything was so much richer than we are used to. I feel I shall not want another meal for a fortnight.

Friends in Scotland are very pleased with themselves because Hess[52] has arrived. I consider it a reflection on their Home Guard, but perhaps they have not any. I am glad people have stopped asking, "What do you think of the arrival of Hess?" They said that for at least a week instead of "What awful weather we are having", as they usually do. My mother says Napoleon's younger brother did the same thing as Hess and suddenly appeared in England in the middle of a campaign.

We are back from Amwell Bury. I had a long walk through the woods there with a local man. There must be a great wood shortage because they are taking hornbeams, fallen trees and standing stumps of trees. Mother has decided the house is too large and will let it as a holiday home for bombed-out women. Patience, Anthea and I were helping her pack up. She and the little girls are going to the Thompsons, a family in the village with children the age of Patience and Anthea. Mrs T is Irish, tall and thin with a lovely complexion and chestnut hair, like a tree fairy. The woods were full of bluebells. They lay like a mauve cloud at the roots of the trees and smelled wonderful.

With love from MR

MAY 28, CHISWICK

My dearest Otto,

Will you tell me if you have grown or got broader or fatter? I have all your clothes here and they are good ones. If you have not grown I will keep them for you, otherwise we can sell them. Clothes are valuable now and will get more so. We might get enough to buy you some new suits.

They have put up eight huts in my mother's field for soldiers, each containing ten men and the poor things have one tap of cold water between them all. The tap is outside, so I do not suppose

---

52    On May 10, 1941, Rudolf Hess, Hitler's Deputy Führer, flew solo from Germany to Scotland on an unauthorised peace mission. He spent the rest of the war under arrest and in 1946 at the Nuremburg Trials was sentenced to life imprisonment.

much washing will go on anyway in winter. Perhaps we will all become like Eskimos and rub ourselves in oil instead of washing. Perhaps we have made too much fuss about being clean.

They are going to ration eggs, which will be good because then we will be able to get them. Up until now we have not had any. I am glad you get plenty of fruit and milk. Eat as much as you can, because it may not last long and one can manage with less food if one has a good foundation, rather like a camel.

With love from MR

MAY 29, CHISWICK

My dearest Otto,

We had letters from Helen and Lawrence today. Helen was thrilled because she had seen the Royal Family. They were supposed to pass the school at 10.30 and arrived at 11.30. All the girls and staff were out to cheer. The carriage passed very close and she saw the Queen and Princesses. In the afternoon they returned and this time she saw the King as well. Helen also marched in a procession of Girl Guides into the town for a service. Of course, it has suddenly dawned on me that it was Empire Day. It seems so far off now. Lawrence wrote about the War Weapons Week procession through Brackley. First came the RAF band ("super"), then the Home Guard, then some "cockeyed" tractor with some "dippy" Land Girls. After this came the local tanks, fire engines and armoured cars (I suppose anything they could get hold of to make the procession longer), then Lawrence and the school. They must all have been out of step, as he complained of kicking the people in front and being kicked by those behind. For a tiny place like Brackley they put up a very good show.

For War Weapons Week in Chiswick, Mrs Stevens went round with a barrel organ and Fred Farrow dressed as a monkey. He climbed lampposts and scratched himself as she played and they made a lot of money. She offered to go as the monkey but refused to climb lampposts, which is fortunate. As the one and only person in the whole of England who has put on weight during the last year (she is now very stout), she has not the figure either for dressing as a monkey or climbing lampposts.

We went to the Royal Academy yesterday for the Summer Exhibition. There were aeroplane pictures by Nevinson, Wilkinson and a man called William Thomas Wood. You will know the pictures of Norman Wilkinson as he did a lot of lovely railway posters. There were, oddly enough, a great many still lives of flowers. There were comparatively few portraits and only two were outstanding, one of a businessman and the other of a Pioneer. There was one of an Orthodox Jew saying his prayers. I should have objected strongly to being painted saying my prayers, but he seemed to be rather enjoying it. One large picture called *The Rescue Party* was of a very beautiful and wonderfully clean lady with red hair being gently lifted up by two godlike young wardens (also very clean). All that appeared to be wrong was a slight tear in her brand-new and very tight mauve jumper. I suppose she had internal injuries. Dame Laura Knight painted a row of cabbages, which was not very inspiring. I thought she might have done onions or lemons instead.

I planted heaps of onions and lettuces the other day. The rain has come and they are growing at last. Also some of the beans are coming up. Do you remember last year we planted two beans in each hole and only one ever came up? Quite a lot have vanished this year, too. We have a bed of artichokes beneath the trees where the washing line runs. I went to Goodban's and bought strong lisle thread for knitting funny thick things like we did in the last war.

I am sorry this letter sounds like a page from Elizabeth Gaskell or Jane Austen, not that it is dull but that it is so very domestic. To finish off I will inform you that Dinah has had kittens at last, two with tails and two without. I have a home for one and can keep another for mousing. I will have to drown the others. Chiswick is full of cats whose people have been evacuated or 'blitzed out'. They are everywhere and have to steal for a living. While we were with Mrs Saunders the other night a fierce fight commenced in the hall between her cat and one of these unwanted strays.

I had a letter from the Home Office today. The application for your release has not gone through. They avoided answering any of my questions and said if you wanted to join up you would have ample opportunity to do so over there.

With love from MR

MAY 31, CHISWICK

My dearest Otto,

The little girls are back for four days, just over the Whitsun holiday. We were asked on the wireless not to bring children into London just now, but my mother is still packing up Amwell Bury and cannot manage with them crashing about all round. Anyway, it is lovely for us having them. We went in to Chiswick today to buy them summer hats, mixed mauves and blues that they can wear with all their clothes and I made Patience a new dress. Tomorrow a great many people are coming to tea to meet them, including a host of Croasdells.

Mrs Saunders is leaving Red Lion House. We have all known her such a long time and will miss not having her to pop in on and talk to. She always seemed to get such odd tenants. The first one was the widow of a famous poet (I forget his name) with a very disagreeable daughter (the one you almost taught German to – I was so relieved when you could not do so). They left Mrs S at the beginning of the war without even bothering to pay their rent. Then she had a doctor and his wife and apparently she was not his wife at all. It made them odd and self-conscious and they would not get to know anyone. Two women came a week ago and seemed frightfully keen on taking the flat. They did not mind an outside lavatory or the dampness of the walls. Then just as they were leaving one of them said, "I hope you will not mind if we bring our little pets." Mrs S asked what these animals were and the woman said, "One is a snake – you will love him, he is sweet and the other is a crocodile. We keep them in nice hot-water tanks." It turned out they were professional fortune-tellers, so they could not have the house anyway as it cannot be let for professional purposes.

I am very jealous of the Owens. They have exactly three pea plants, each covered in blooms. I have rows and rows of pea plants and not a flower among them.

With love from MR

My dearest Otto,

I had the children taken by Polyfoto at Selfridges yesterday and asked about sending the snaps abroad to you.

It is very cold and wet in Europe and has been the worst winter in Russia for 250 years. I wish the Russians would keep their beastly weather to themselves. I am afraid that like their ballet and their government, it is liable to spread.

Peggy Owen's husband goes back to camp today. Fortunately for Peggy, she had her wedding before the clothes rationing came in so is set up for years. The rationing of garments broke like a thunderclap. It had not leaked out and no one could lay aside stocks of stuff. At the moment if we need new clothes we have to hand in our margarine cards. For Helen it is all right because she and I can wear the same things. Lawrence will need all his coupons for trousers. He will wear out six pairs this year.

Ilse is back from a weekend holiday and brought me a big spring onion. I have dug up a lot more lawn and planted out my lettuce. Myra insisted on thinning out my peas, much to my annoyance. Digging the lawn is such hard work and makes one so frightfully tired.

Gerald Spencer Pryce suddenly appeared for lunch the other day, much to my joy and Teddy's annoyance. He came to see his bombed house, which the council are trying to pull down so as to widen the road. I'm glad to say he has stopped that. Mr S P is not nice and I would not trust him beyond my nose, but I like him all the same. He is clever and tells one interesting and amusing things. He has been abroad for the government on a mission to establish friendship with the United States. He was always keen on that subject.

With love from MR

My dearest Otto,

Things here have been quiet lately in every way, except last night when we were woken by a terrific bang. It was not near although it was so loud.

All the vegetables have been rejoicing in the rain and now it is a beautiful day. It is wonderful to have the sun again and makes one feel quite different. I am eating some of our spring greens this weekend. I gave one shilling's worth to Mr Morley and to Mr Croasdell and I have exactly one shilling's worth to eat. I have often wondered how much one saves in money by growing one's own food. I think lettuce and tomatoes save a lot and most things grown from seeds, but bought plants save nothing at all. The cabbage plants I bought have not quite covered what I gave for them and the leaves are so tough they need more gas to cook them than those from the grocer's.

Ilse, Miss Coverley and I had arranged to take tea to Kew. It was fine until we got there and then it simply poured with rain, with thunder and lightning. We spent most of the time in the waterlily house, which was lovely and warm. When it cleared we had tea on a wet bench among the azaleas. Other people followed our example and soon the lovely flowers were surrounded by unlovely picnickers.

I bought some soap the other day as we hear it is to be rationed. They say coke will be impossible to get next year, so we shall have to learn to splash about in the basin. That is all right for grown-ups, but how could Patience be kept clean by a basinful of water? She really needs about three baths a day.

With love from MR

JUNE 10, CHISWICK

My dearest Otto,

It is so cold that Ilse and I have two eiderdowns on our beds at night. I am having a horrid time with clothes coupons. Helen has gone through hers in nine days. How funny your getting that 10/- I sent to Huyton. I thought it had gone for good. There are still several cakes of soap, some bath towels, two face towels, some underclothes and two books trailing you about the world. The books were one Dickens and one Thackeray.

I am told some new people have come to Oak Cottage in the Mall, a doctor and his very fat, smart and much made-up wife. If she is really so fat I do not see how she will be able to get into Oak Cottage, which is so small. It is supposed to be the dampest house in Chiswick, so I cannot think the poor woman will manage to remain very smart for long. Actually, our house may be the dampest now. All the rooms on the top storey are leaking. Most of us sleep up there and I had to take down one of my pictures because a large crop of mushrooms was growing on the back.

*continued the next day*

*Molly and Ilse at The Clarendon,*
*a pub of dubious repute.*

I went to meet Ilse and her cousin Berndt last night. He is a nice, steady lad. It is always a good thing to know people's relations. Myra and I both would have been in lunatic asylums by now if we had not known each other. I met them at Hammersmith Broadway and meant to give them coffee, but nothing was open so I barged them into The Clarendon, where I had never dared go before. Did you ever read A.P. Herbert's book *The Water Gipsies*? It is about people who lived in a barge on Chiswick Mall and is very clever and amusing and sometimes horrid. In it the young man takes the girls to The Clarendon and I had always wanted to see what it was like. Inside it is all cream and plush with an enormous bar along one side of the room. There were masses of men standing around, all rather stout with big tummies. I did not know there were so many of that type in the world before, let alone in Hammersmith. A lot of very fair and rather doubtful-looking ladies were entertaining soldiers and I was sorry because the boys were all so young and should have had mothers and proper young ladies to be walking out with. There were also some respectable elderly couples who had apparently come in to see 'life'. I did not think the surroundings quite suitable for Ilse but it was out of the rain. Must stop.

With love from MR

JUNE 13, CHISWICK

My dearest Otto,

We had a food parcel from Uncle Edward's sister in Trinidad yesterday. Tea (in a lovely Chinese box, only it had burst open), marmalade (which is priceless), sugar (which I shall use for jam) and a lovely big tin of butter that I will keep for the holidays. We felt rather bad about it because from what she says they have less to eat than we have here.

It is early morning and the sun is silvery and just warm. We had another noisy night. They said one big bomber was losing height as it passed over us and might have been brought down. I heard it getting very low and knew I should get out of bed to look at it, but I was too sleepy.

Fred Farrow leaves the ARP and goes into the Army next week. Everyone is depressed about it. We do not want to be left to Bill Bryant, our head warden, who loses his head at the mere smell of a bomb in the distance. Fred put in for the Navy as he has been to sea, but they stuck him down as Army by mistake.

With love from MR

JUNE 15, CHISWICK

My dearest Otto,

I went to the ballet on Thursday with the Croasdells and enjoyed it so much. It is the first time I have done anything of that sort in almost a year and I should not have gone if they had not more or less pulled me out.

On Friday I took my ponyskin coat to cold storage. Then I went to Kew and shared sandwiches with a white duck with three yellow babies, a brown duck with five brown babies and a pair of geese who swore horribly as I came near their two fluffy grey goslings. There were only a few old men in the gardens, no one else and though it was lovely I got frightfully depressed being alone and had to go home.

We went to Mrs Volkov last night to see the picture of Tata, her cook, done by Mr Austin. She is a Cossack with a lovely face and beautiful colouring. I suppose it is very clever, but he had drawn her sitting on a chair, quite straight, with her feet in front of her. The result is that her feet and legs look huge and her head is tiny. It is right that the feet should be larger than the head, because they are much nearer to the artist with the model sitting in that position, but they were the biggest part of the picture and made it look all wrong.

Dreadful things have been happening to our animals. First Dinah killed Miss C's canary as it was bathing in its saucer in front of the fire. Then a tomcat got in by the tree outside the drawing-room window and fought with Dinah, leaving clumps of fur all over the place. After breakfast her kitten disappeared and we think it was taken by the tomcat and killed. Dinah is very hard-hearted and does not seem to mind. Perhaps she has hidden the baby and goes out now and again to feed it. We are longing to hear something definite about your plans.

With love from MR

My dearest Otto,

We are having summer at last. Last week I bought a pair of dungarees in Hammersmith. You can get them without coupons. They are cotton, wash well and look nicer than slacks. If you are thin slacks won't keep up properly and if you are fat you look awful in them. Ilse and I went to buy her a cotton frock and went all through Hammersmith without finding one. The cotton must all be needed for bandages.

Afterwards we went to tea with the Drews. He is about 33 and wears a very exciting-looking beard. She is about 24. They have had a baby for ten weeks now, but do not know how to cope with the poor little thing. They won't hold its head in the right way and it flops all over the place. They gave it tomato juice in a bottle too fast and the little creature had hiccups. Instead of patting it on the back, they gave it water in a bottle. I thought they might burst it. However, it had its revenge in a way usual with infants, much to the embarrassment of its father. Mother did not mind in the least, which makes me think more than ever that we go back to the animal if we are not careful. Mrs Drew reminds me exactly of Dinah in her attitude to her young. We still have not found her kitten.

Mr. D used to play the piano before the war, learning from a clever young man who played at The Promenade concerts. He is now scrubbing floors in the Army and is heartbroken as he thinks his hands will never be any good again. One of his co-scrubbers is also a musician, so between them they hope to give concerts for the men. It seems odd that when they are always crying out for people to entertain troops and factory hands that they let two good musicians scrub floors and send round vulgar comedians instead. It makes me wild to see people being given the bad and the indifferent when they have a right to the best.

I wish I knew what was happening to you.

With love from MR

My dearest Otto,

It looks as if war will break out between the US and Germany or the US and Japan very soon. If it does we will be cut off from Australia except for cables and clipper mails. I wonder what they will do with you. My child, I am so very anxious for you. I am sending you my sisters' addresses in Kenya. Many of the troops moving up to North Africa pass Avril's farm in Sotik, so there may be a chance of your passing it too, one day. My other sister, Nancy, lives outside Nairobi. She has not been there much since her husband was killed, but you will be able to find out about her from the two cinemas she runs. There are only three in town, I think.

I went to see *Gone With The Wind*[53] today with Mrs Chandler. The first part was horrid, just like the Germans walking into Poland. I suppose all invasions are the same. After that the story changed and became that of a woman who made up her mind she was going to have all the best she could out of life whatever the cost. After every war there are those of us who decide on this course of action. It broke down for her as it always does and it made an interesting psychological study. I was glad to have seen it, because I had got all wound up and bothered about things and the film made me think of other things and now I can see a bit straighter than I could before I went out.

Something very big has just exploded not far off and we are wondering what it was. It cannot have been a bomb as there are no planes anywhere about.

---

53   The film of *Gone with the Wind*, Margaret Mitchell's famous novel, opened in London in April 1941 and ran for three years.

We have workmen all over the house repainting it. For a vicarage one pays so much every year and at the end of five years the money is taken out and used to do up the outside of the house. If it costs more than the money put aside, the vicar has to make up the difference. We have had a bother making the dilapidations fit the money in hand, but it is a good thing the work is done now and not next year, as prices are rising so much.

There are all sorts of rumours about this war, but it is no good telling you them because by the time you get this they will be rumours no longer, having become either facts or merely fancy. They say in tonight's paper that 62 internees are on their way back from Australia, mostly ill or married people. What a pity you are not either ill or married.

They have opened several hostels in this neighbourhood under the Red Cross. Some, like the one at Greenash, for 'shocked' people and some for grass-widowers. The latter are men whose wives are away, presumably evacuated with the children. My husband has been made a Red Cross Chaplain to look after them all. He is supposed to have a very snappy uniform, but although it was ordered ages ago it has not yet materialised. The run on cloth for uniforms has been so great that there is not enough left even for armlets. I think it is silly to make him have a uniform merely for visiting rest centres, when if he was allowed to wear his medal ribbons on his ordinary clothes and an armlet, everyone would know what he was.

We went to the opening of one of the grass-widower homes last week in Sutton Court Road. It was like a musical comedy. Twelve people stood in a semicircle and each spoke for a few minutes thanking everyone else for what they had done. They were all good speakers and liked the sound of their own voices and enjoyed themselves very much. Afterwards the listeners were rewarded for their patience with sandwiches and tea. I saw Chiswick's very energetic Mayor and Mayoress. She is pretty, young, clever, dresses well and writes beauty hints in women's magazines. He is much older (50 to her 37, I think) and stout, very red and much like a hot egg to look at.

The other day my husband came in frightfully excited and said Underhill [the Bishop of Bath and Wells] had said the destruction of our lovely old buildings was worse than the loss of life in air raids. Uncle Edward said he had always thought that himself, but when I asked him if he would rather lose St Paul's Cathedral or Lawrence, he refused to answer so I knew what he meant. Teddy would certainly send St Paul's and everything else crashing to earth rather than let Lawrence get a scratch in an air raid, which shows that one person can actually have two perfectly right opinions about one thing. Then there is another interesting side to that question of values. If something is absolutely beautiful, will it ever pass away completely? I think great beauty must leave something behind even if it is what we call 'destroyed'.

With love from MR


JUNE 23, CHISWICK

My dearest Otto,

We heard this morning that Germany has marched on Russia. Someone once told me that fighting Russia was like battling a feather pillow of immense size. Hitler already occupies Finland and Romania. I think the Poles will help him in their Russian-occupied territory, all except the Jewish Poles, though there are not many of them left. What a queer muddle it all is. The sun is lovely and the whole earth so golden, green and beautiful, it seems impossible that there should be so much misery.

We went to see mother and the little girls yesterday. They have all settled happily in their new quarters with Mrs Thompson. I was afraid my mother would be unhappy in someone else's house, but she goes back to the big house every day after the children have gone to school and works in the drawing room, which she has kept for herself. She is running her garden as a market garden and selling everything. She has made friends with the matron and does not mind the house being let because it is giving so much pleasure to so many people.

I bought gooseberries from the garden and planned to make jam today, but found the sugar sent from Trinidad to have broken loose like the tea. It was mingled with both tea leaves and oil. Even so

I could not waste it, so I made the jam. It smells odd and oily but tastes quite nice and having the tea in amongst the sugar has made the jam a nice rich brown.

There is very little lawn left to cut these days as we have dug up so much. Gem arrives tomorrow and we are prepared to hear Dennis (Silk Pyjamas) discussed solidly for six hours as she is spending this weekend with him. Miss Coverley is away so I shall probably get the whole force of the explosion. Poor Gem, I hope she will be happy. I think they should marry soon, otherwise he will be sent abroad and she may never see him again.

I want to get someone to come to live in this house, or perhaps a couple, leaving me free to make munitions. The difficulty is I should never get one person or even two to do all that I do.

With love from MR

JULY 2, CHISWICK

My dearest Otto,

We are having such lovely weather. We have all our meals out, even breakfast and last night I took the shelter bed out and slept under the fig tree. It is like being in a green tent and the leaves are so thick the sun does not get up in your face as usually happens when one sleeps without a roof over one's head.

I am very proud of my vegetables. I think mine is the best amateur garden about here. We eat masses of lettuce and I have enough to give away. We have had spinach twice and I am hoping for peas on Sunday. I must say there is a depressing resemblance in all these amateur gardens. The owners proudly show you a row of carrots (spindly), lettuce (the birds have taken most of these), turnips (but none of the family will eat them), cabbage (eaten by caterpillars), beans (the pigeons love them) and tomatoes (very late this year and showing no signs of flowers yet). I hope by the time this war is over we will all be experts at gardening. It is wonderful to go into a garden like my mother's, which is run by a professional and see things growing as they should, all in rotation.

I am now reading *Gone With The Wind*. It is especially interesting at this time as it tells of the downfall of a civilisation. I expect the descriptions of the Southern States after they are sacked by the Yankees is a good account of what happens in every country when it has been overrun by another. What is also interesting is how the Southerners found themselves starving and without homes and had to start again. They had been lawyers and doctors and slave owners and had to become builders and storekeepers and road menders. They gradually used their other faculties and some of them rose to the top again, some remained where they were and some sank right down. It is just like what is happening to people today.

With love from MR

JULY 4, CHISWICK

My dearest Otto,

A wonderful thing has happened. Ilse has been teaching me German and I finally understand about accusatives and things. It came to me quite suddenly and I can't think why I did not understand it before.

Anthea and Patience are leaving Ware Grammar School next term as there are 40 children in Patience's class and 25 in Anthea's and they are not getting enough teaching. Also a lot of the children are very rough and Anthea gets knocked about because she is more gentle than the others. Patience can hold her own with the roughest, but I do not know if it is a very good thing. They are also leaving Mrs Thompson after only a month, because her cook (an evacuee from the coast) is allowed to go home and it is too much work for Mrs T.

For the following term my mother and the little girls will go back to Amwell Bury as boarders, because during the colder months there are not many people needing holidays and they want to make the house pay. It all sounds very odd, but the Dunlops, who live at the end of the Amwell Bury drive, are already boarders in their own house, which has been taken over by bombed babies. One of my aunts lives in half of her own house and the rest is a hospital. Then they will move to a cottage on the estate that Mother is having done up called Tollgate[54]. Mrs Nichols, who lives in Amwell Bury Lodge, will walk up every day to do the cooking.

Gem's young man, Silk Pyjamas, is getting 48 hours next week. I wonder if all this short leave has something to do with Russia[55]. I see in the papers today that we are soon to be allies, so perhaps I shall be able to learn 'The Red Flag', which I have always wanted to know.

I have been busy getting the blackout ready, as it gets dark early now. This year I am reopening the drawing room because it is so much nicer than the dining room and if any sun comes it will need less fuel for heating. Coal will be scarce, so it is a consideration. Of course I will have to black out the windows. I have opened out the room next to Ilse's room for Helen and had a horrid time with a bed that got stuck in the door frame and took a large piece out of the wall. I hope that Helen will marry very young so that when she is my age she will have a son of your age to help with these sorts of things.

With love from a very cross, disappointed, hot and annoyed MR

JULY 15, CHISWICK

My dearest Otto,

I have another girl in the house now – Irene from Latvia, very fair and shy. She is waiting for her 'call up' for the ATS [Auxiliary Territorial Service]. Her father was a doctor and both her parents are dead. She has two little sisters in Latvia with an aunt. She was studying in England when the war broke out and was stuck here. She is particularly unhappy about something but I do not know what yet.

The house is simply bursting with girls. I might just as well be keeping a girls' school. I am so glad Lawrence will be back in a few

---

54   The house was named for the tollgate mentioned in 'The Diverting History of John Gilpin', a comic ballad published in 1782 by William Cowper that describes a merchant's wild ride on a bolting horse between London and Ware.

55   Germany invaded Russia, its former ally, on June 22, 1941.

days to give a little comic relief to the situation. It is nearly a year since you left.

Did I tell you the latest about Mrs Saunders? We had all keyed ourselves up for her departure from Red Lion House when suddenly she made some arrangement with the brewery to stay on (they own the house). She will store her furniture in part of it and shut up the top storey, which is too damp to stay in and live on the ground floor.

Miss Coverley has taken some amusing snaps of us all in the garden. I wish I could send them to you. There is one wonderful one of Uncle Edward and me looking like film stars, smiling at one another in the approved style.

The Elwells had a nephew staying with them last night. He is up to get a bar to his DSO [Distinguished Service Order] and they are going to Buckingham Palace today. We all met at the Nelsons to celebrate and Mary gave us queer drinks in oddly assorted glasses (if you break a glass these days it is difficult to replace). Tom Nelson keeps bees and had been stung on his foot. He insisted on taking off his shoes and socks and we all had to look to see if any stings had been left in (there had not). He is such a funny shape, with no waist, that he cannot bend far enough to see for himself.

With love from MR

*Molly examining Tom Nelson's foot for bee stings.*

*Molly at her typewriter with Edward in the garden.*

My dearest Otto,

Irene does not come from Latvia but from Estonia, which I think means the 'stony land'. She helps me with the house and it makes a lot of difference having someone to take a couple of rooms and do them every day. Because it has been so very quiet – no bombs lately – we have got all the beds up out of the cellar. Mr Morley brought them up for me last night. The mattresses are covered with mushrooms and the blankets are filthy from being used on the ground in the brewery shelter. They are now all airing in the garden, which looks like an old clothes shop.

This morning we went to the Estonian Legation to get in touch with Irene's people, but nothing could be done about cabling or writing as no one yet knows if Estonia belongs to Russia or Germany. If it becomes German she will be able to write via the British Red Cross. If Russian she will not be able to write at all. She has relations in both countries and I am afraid they will all have a very bad time whatever happens.

Irene and Ilse do not get on well together as they are completely different types. Ilse is fair and fluffy, all pretty face and not much brain and Irene is not pretty but intelligent and strong-willed. They walk stiffly round each other like two little dogs that might begin to fight at any moment.

My best hat died on my head during a thunderstorm a fortnight ago and Ilse is to make me a new one, though she has no time and is rather slow anyway. I am wearing a turban that I think looks all right.

Did I tell you that I still have your fountain pen? I am glad as they are almost impossible to buy now and even if it is not going very well I shall be able to put it right for you when all this is over.

With love from MR

My dearest Otto,

Yesterday was Helen's first day home and we took tea to Kew Gardens. Lawrence is also back. Last night he and Gem slept out under the fig tree but had to come in at 6 am when it started raining, with thunder crashing and lightning flashing all round. I did an enormous bout of cooking, four meals for eight people. Lawrence has developed a huge, ultra-English appetite. I have a new boy, Hans, 18, with a very small, Continental appetite. He was sent out from Berlin four years ago by a society saving children and has been at a school in Wells where he was very happy. He is with us only a few days before going on to study civil engineering at the Poly, which of course is evacuated to the countryside. He will get on all right. He is clever, with nice manners and looks just like an English boy.

*continued next day*

This is written Sunday, 24 hours later. It has been pouring for the last 12 hours and so this morning I pushed the children off to see Chiswick House. There are some lovely roses there and as Hans has lived the last four years of his life in a boys' school and Helen and Irene the last four in a girls' school, it is good for them to learn how to talk to each other. Lawrence is a comic touch in the middle.

I took Irene round London last week, more or less what you and I did last year. It was horrid how things have changed so much. The children are back and there is such a noise in the house at the moment I can't write properly. I will try again soon.

With love from MR

My dearest Otto,

We are in the middle of the holidays and I have five children of various nationalities, aged 8 to 18, in the house, also the usual crowds of grown-ups coming and going. Thinking of large and filling meals becomes a real problem and in the end we shall become like the Chinese and live on rice, which so far is unrationed and very filling.

Today all the children except Ilse (who is working) went to the pictures. The film, *Pimpernel Smith*[56], was about concentration camps, so I could not go. Ilse could not have gone either, but the rest of them are too young to mind. Even Hans and Irene do not seem to understand about them. It is now getting on for 11 pm and Hans has not yet turned up. I hope he has not fallen asleep in the theatre. I am always in a fuss because of the curfew[57].

We had a man to lunch who told me my leeks were planted wrong and that I had to dig them up and replant each one. They have to be put in a deep hole that you fill with water. You do not replace the earth. In time the leeks swell and fill the hole up with themselves. I hope he is right. I have had a box of very successful cress, which I planted for Ilse's sandwiches, though it is difficult to cut and in the end I had to pull it up by the roots. We had an air raid the other night. Everyone was quite surprised as we have not had one for so long.

With love from MR

AUGUST 3, CHISWICK

My dearest Otto,

One wonders how long Japan will remain out of all this. Each week brings the Sunday papers with 'scare headlines' about their troop movements.

Lawrence and I went on the island last week. The tide has been very low, so we had quite a long time there. It is covered with willows that grow thickly together and it is warm and wet and smells rather like a greenhouse. It reminded me of the part of Uganda where Dick and I once stayed. L and I went down a wriggly path in the centre

---

56 *Pimpernel Smith* was produced by its star, Leslie Howard, known for *Gone with the Wind* and *The Scarlet Pimpernel*. The story, about an Englishman who saves Jews from camps in pre-war Germany, is said to have inspired Raoul Wallenberg's rescue of Jews in Sweden. Howard died on 1 June 1943, aboard a civilian plane shot down by the Luftwaffe.

57 Aliens had a curfew of 10.30 pm to 6 am.

of the island through bushes and flowers. At the end we climbed down the sticky mud bank and crossed the river, which was just a trickle, by some stepping-stones. At least Lawrence did, I was wearing rubber boots and waded over. You can walk all along that bank of the river now and see the places where there once was a landing stage for a boat at the end of each garden.

The house is suddenly very quiet. Helen has gone to the country and Lawrence, Fred, Tasher, Irene and Miss Coverley are all out. Hans is writing many letters, with many sighs and scrapings of chair. Ilse is cleaning her room and occasionally I hear thumps and bumps. Bonzo is fast asleep on the best sofa, the broken one that is nailed up so I cannot have the cover taken off to wash it. He knows he should not be there and keeps looking out of the corner of his eye to see if I have seen him. If he thinks I have noticed him he closes his eyes tight, because he thinks if he can't see me I certainly can't see him.

With love from MR

AUGUST 10, CHISWICK

My dearest Otto,

Myra has heard that internees who join the Pioneers are to be sent back to England. Do join up. I'm so afraid if you get released and choose to stay on for farm work in Australia you will be stuck there forever. It is funny that directly I make up my mind that you have gone for good and get used to the idea, something happens and we think you may come home after all. I still think a lot will depend on the Japanese.

Teddy and Lawrence are painting the bathroom. They have managed to make the whole house reek of paint and there is paint on everything everywhere. One cannot have a bath, or even wash one's hands in the bathroom, or walk down the passage because of all the bottles and soap and towels that have been put there. I hope it will be over soon. Anyway they are enjoying it all very much and although it is costing a lot they would not have derived nearly so much pleasure if they had spent the money on theatre tickets or some other entertainment.

*Edward and Lawrence painting the bathroom.*

All's well here. I heard today that Englishwomen up to age 60 may have to register, so you may find me marching about in uniform one of these days. I hope I will be allowed to wear a Glengarry hat. I am so excited now there seems another chance of your coming back. I am sure you should join up. I have still got the wool if you need socks, but the others ate your marmalade. I let them have it when I thought there was no hope of your return.

With love from MR

AUGUST 17, CHISWICK

My dearest Otto,

We are all very pleased about the meeting of Roosevelt and Churchill[58]. It is what a lot of people have been hoping for for

---

58   The Atlantic Charter, announced by Churchill and Roosevelt on August 14, 1941, established guidelines for postwar settlement.

some time. We also had a broadcast from the Queen. She speaks so nicely and simply. I like listening to her, although she always begins by being so frightened. Actually I think this helps to make her effective, because one knows exactly how she is feeling. We also had a brilliant broadcast from Dorothy Thompson[59]. I have listened to many excellent women speakers – in fact I think the average woman is a much better speaker than the average man – but DT is much the best I have ever heard. She has a nice voice, with just enough American accent to give it 'punch' and her words pour forth without any hesitation.

I had an awful time getting everyone off from the Vicarage this morning, I had to cut 48 sandwiches. I am so good at it now I can almost cut them in my sleep. First we pushed Ilse off, then Lawrence and my husband, then Irene, who was going for a shorthand course for the first time and feeling rather groggy about it. I am longing to know how she got on. I am getting troops of women in to help with the housework because I'm getting so thin and have so many wrinkles and grey hairs I think I must be overworking. The difficulty is to fix it so that they will not meet and fight with each other. I want to help with the babies in the crèche round the corner in the autumn. They are having to refuse babies because there are not enough people to look after them. I went to see them the other day. They are so sweet.

With love from MR

AUGUST 26, CHISWICK

My dearest Otto,

We have returned from visiting my mother and the little girls in Amwell Bury. Teddy and I stayed over the field at Rookery House, my brother Ralph's house. We had awful weather, with rain almost all the time. It was sad to see the crops, which were so good, all but

---

59   American journalist and radio broadcaster Dorothy Thompson was as well-known and influential as Eleanor Roosevelt.

in the wet. The house is very old. It used to be the coaching inn on the main London to Cambridge road. After the days of coaches they shifted the road to avoid a hill and now it lies up a quiet leafy lane. It is a fascinating house, with unexpected stairs and corners and inglenooks. The chimneys are so huge, you can see the light coming in from the roof. Dick Turpin, the famous highwayman, is supposed to have hidden in one.

The children built a house for themselves in the wood using the roof of an Army lorry that had broken up in a collision. They used an old zebra skin of my brother's by way of a floor, then put in a 'stove' and cooked a dreadful and very dirty meal amidst a cloud of smoke. I'm sorry to say we had to eat the meal.

Amwell Bury was, as usual, full of old ladies having holidays. They all seemed so happy and sat in the garden in spite of the damp. If one goes for a walk in the woods, one suddenly comes upon three or four of them crashing through the undergrowth. They are all so amusing and kind. The English poor have a wonderful sense of humour, which is very useful. They joke about things that would completely knock them out if they could not see the funny side.

At the end of the week I had to return to Chiswick as Anthea is in quarantine for chickenpox. Patience is all right, but I have both the little girls here, as they are happier together. They are both looking like young lions with immense mops of hair. I am taking Patience for a haircut this afternoon, but poor Anthea cannot yet go into shops so will have to continue with her mane a little longer. The rest of the family are already off to my Aunt Maude's cottage in Sandbanks, in Dorset. She has lent it to us for a holiday. Teddy wrote yesterday to say their cook failed them at the last moment and their diet is a little monotonous. Helen is good at sausages and I think they can all make tea, but there it ends. They have lunch at a hotel, so at least there is one good meal each day.

With love from MR

My dearest Otto,

Anthea is now out of quarantine and this is the last weekend before we join Teddy, Lawrence and Helen in Sandbanks. Soon I shall be in a modern bungalow by the sea – very different. I am not looking forward to the journey. We can go from Chiswick Station straight to Waterloo and book through to Bournemouth, which makes things easy, but I hear the trains are crowded. I have not been by train since the commencement of the war. One of the mysterious things is why trains should be so crowded directly there is a war. There are the same trains and the same amount of people in the country and no one travels unless they can help it, but the trains always get crowded all the same. I remember in the last war when we went up to London we always made for the milk van, because we knew it was the only place where there would be any room. We always had to stand all the way, but we rather enjoyed it as our friends went by the milk van too and it was more fun than being stuck stiffly in seats at each side of a carriage.

Irene's sister has arrived for a visit. She is very beautiful – really lovely, not just pretty – with a round face and light brown hair full of life and colour. She has wonderful grey eyes and a rather funny pushed-in mouth. Unfortunately, like all girls who do hard work, she stoops badly. She is learning gardening and taking it up scientifically, which means she will learn all about the propagation of plants, grafting and pruning and hybrids and all about seeds and fertilisation. It is knowing as much about plants as a doctor knows about human beings. She is a very nice girl and speaks perfect English with a tiny Scotch accent. My poor Irene has been landed without any looks and I think perhaps her bad manner may be the result of an inferiority complex. She is one of only two difficult refugees I have ever had and so I must think myself lucky, as in the last 18 months 17 have passed through this house: four English, four Belgians, five Austrians, two Estonians, two Germans.

I am rather worried about Ilse as well as Irene. They will have to register for war work next week and I am so afraid they may be called up while I am away and sent to the North of England where they don't know anyone. Anne Croasdell, who is pretty hardy and much older, had such an awful time when she was on government work. All the girls stayed out till midnight and got drunk and just ran about as they thought fit. And they were shovelled into billets where the people did not want them or look after them. I can't think of Ilse in a billet and can imagine it only too well with Irene. Thank heavens that Helen is not old enough to be called up.

Irene and her sister and the little girls are going to Kew this afternoon, taking tea with them. They said something about a boat and I only hope they don't drown.

My old ration book has turned up, thank goodness, so I shall be able to get my clothes coupons. I thought I should have to go about like an ancient Briton till the end of the war.

The Sunday paper has no scare headlines about the Japs today, so I feel they will probably attack someone quite soon. I have been busy adding great chunks of fabric onto Lawrence's pyjamas. He has grown out of them and only has enough coupons left for one pair of new ones.

Well that is all the news. I hope quite soon to hear what is happening to you.

With love from MR

SEPTEMBER 8, CHISWICK

My dearest Otto,

We have just come back from our holiday at Sandbanks. It is beautiful, with dunes of pale gold rising from mauve heather. It is as if a giant had upset great sackfuls of gold in heaps on a mauve carpet. In the more sheltered spots are tiny woods of fir trees all blown into queer shapes and stunted by the wind. My aunt's house is quite near the cottage and has a wonderful garden. There are 'red hot pokers', which do really look like pokers, with scarlet pens standing up very still, just wonderful against the dark and gloomy firs. She also has scented white lilies with coloured spots on their petals. The garden runs down to the sea and we could watch the ships from there. It gives one an idea of what we owe to the Navy.

The wireless and newsreels tell us about ships taking food across the ocean, but as we are an unimaginative people we understand more readily by seeing for ourselves. I do not think people would be greedy or pinch rations if they really knew what was going on.

Lawrence has just come in with a handful of sticky figs we brought back, which he says are ripe. They are nasty, but even so I must try to make jam out of them. This will be the first year that my aunt's tree has ever produced eatable fruit. One of our chief topics of conversation in summers there is 'why the figs never ripen', so we will have to think of something else to discuss instead.

We got a wonderful parcel of food from America yesterday: dried peaches and prunes, lemon juice, brown sugar and a very exciting thing sewn up into a small, greasy sack that we have not yet dared open. I am still busy adding to all the children's clothes and hope to make them all last another 12 months.

I took the children to Richmond yesterday to hire a boat. There are a lot of lovely weeping willow trees bending down to touch the water and a little island round which one can go. The town stands on a hilly bank and looks so picturesque from the water.

We started off with a fierce argument with the owners of the boat, because being Scotch, I did not think they should charge 3/- per hour for a boat to hold six people when they were mostly children and did not take up as much room as even three fat old men. In the end we took a rowing boat and all the children had ten minutes' rowing in turn. We had one anxious moment when a pleasure steamer about 30 times as large as ourselves came bearing swiftly down upon us when Patience was rowing. However, it was all right. All sorts of people were on the water, including two smartly dressed ladies with kid gloves, which did not seem very suitable for rowing.

Several old men were sitting so silent and still at the side of the water that we thought they were dead, until we noticed their fishing rods. I think people fish because we live in such a noisy, mechanical age that one cannot live a life of contemplation. The folk who in the Middle Ages would have gone into a monastery now take up fishing.

*continued September 11*

This is being written three days later. I now have two more evacuees in the house, English this time, in Alice's old room where the Adamses were. The young man has come out of hospital and his wife is expecting a baby. They are completely on the rocks, everything pawned to pay expenses. They have been in shelters for a fortnight and the first thing he asked for was a wash. He has a job, thank God and is starting work tomorrow.

*continued September 12*

The dear little English couple I told you about decamped in the middle of the night, taking four blankets and an alarm clock with them. We had the police up and they could do nothing about it, but they did tell me that they had my great-grandmother's silver teapot at the station. It had been stolen about a month ago. I shall be glad to get it back. I often wonder why the English are such thieves, because we are a rich nation and have wonderful social services. I think it is a love of adventure. The English make wonderful airmen and explorers because they are fearless without much imagination. It is only exciting to loot houses and steal from rest centres if one cannot understand how the victims will feel. Most of us lead frightfully dull lives, with nothing more exciting than the cinema.

*A young couple given shelter at the Vicarage made off in the middle of the night, taking four blankets and an alarm clock.*

I have a very strong feeling that something special is happening to you. I wish I knew what it is. I am so afraid you will be sent out East. I had better stop because of the weight of the letter. God bless you my child.

With love from MR

OCTOBER 18, CHISWICK

My dearest Otto,

My mother heard from the War Office that Dick was killed last autumn. There had been some muddle and three men had been buried without their identification disks being taken off. Dick was one of them. They found out from prisoners. At least he died in clean open desert land, the sort of country he loved. I had rather that happened to him a thousand times than have him live under Nazi rule. After all, death has to come to us all and what matters is the way we die. I am sorry, I did not mean to begin thinking out loud into the typewriter. Anyway I must go and do the shopping. I will also go around to the crèche again to see if they want my help with the babies. There is such a lot to do in this house but it is not war work, which I would prefer and might even find less strenuous.

I am now looking after a boy of 20 called Herbert. He was interned in Canada for a long time and has put down his name for the Pioneers. The Quaker relief agency rang me up because they did not want him to go to a hostel. This house is full, but I have billeted him nearby and he spends his days here. He is a nice boy.

Last Sunday we had rather an exciting time because two bishops came. The new Bishop of London in the morning and the Bishop of Kensington in the afternoon. It was a great pity they came together, but it could not be helped. Fortunately everyone likes to hear the Bishop of Kensington, so most of them actually turned out three times that day to church, early morning, late morning and afternoon. It was the first time the Bishop of London had been here. He is trying to go around and visit all the churches in his diocese and says it will take him five years to do so.

With love from MR

**Molly learns that Otto is at last returning to England.**

My dearest Otto,

I have been given this address as one that may find you. I heard a rumour that some Pioneers from Australia had arrived and I rushed up to London to start on a tour of Committees. I expected it to take the whole day but quickly learned that your transport left Sydney in October. I got such a surprise and felt all queer.

I do not think you can be home much before the middle of December. I imagine your boat had to wait and join with a convoy before you could cross. I'm told that if you join up you will be sent to a camp in the Isle of Man, where you can apply to be posted to any company of the Pioneers you wish. You will probably like to stay with the men you come home with. All Pioneers seem to be a great way from London, but I think that is as well. They say you are to get leave almost at once. I wish you could come home for Christmas, but that is too much to hope for. Everyone here is longing to see you. I'm afraid my children will be very disappointed if you come back while they are all away at school.

The last 18 months have been ghastly. Do you know, I look old enough to be your grandmother instead of your mother. You had the other side of the picture and I know your experience was worse than Myra's and mine. I hope and pray that you and she will have got through the worst part of your lives while you are young. I know you are both strong and brave enough to start building a better world out of your experiences.

With love from MR

**Two months later, Otto is back in England, on the Isle of Man.**

My dearest Otto,

I was so thankful to get your letter yesterday. No one seems to know why you are in the Isle of Man. The Pioneer recruiting officer is enquiring. I am afraid, my child, that you face many more months of internment. You know how slow things are. It is ghastly not knowing what to do. I must say this last development did take me by surprise. I never thought they would intern you again after bringing you all the way back across the world. I do not see why you, who were put in prison by Nazis and who hold a Jewish passport and passed 'C' by the tribunal should be shut up, while Herbert and lots of other people who the Nazis did not bother to hunt down and who have German passports and were passed 'B' at their tribunals are allowed to join up and do all sorts of things without any question. It is all most bewildering and very alarming. I suppose I should be thankful, because ordinarily at your age you would have been abroad in the Army or a prisoner in enemy hands.

I will tell you all about Myra. She has fallen on her feet at last. She has a job in London at a leather-goods firm with very nice people. Although she has only been there a few weeks she has already had a 'rise'. She is living in a house that has been turned into 'rooms'. The address is 19 Endsleigh Street WC1 and her telephone number Euston 2462. She knows other people in the house and goes to supper every evening to friends who live near, so she gets proper food. It is the one saving thing. I think she could not have gone through the disappointment of your not coming home if she had still been at the old work.

This last week has otherwise been just awful. Irene has finished her typing course and worries because she cannot get work, my husband is worried about his work and I am worried about you. I lose everything I lay hands on. This week I have lost a pearl necklace, a pair of earrings, a 10/- note, an important book and a whole lot of little things as well. Most of these things have turned up again in perfectly silly places.

The children are coming back soon. I wish Helen were here now. She is just old enough to understand things but not old enough to take them in, so I can tell her my troubles and she sympathises and it does not bother her. I can't tell anyone else, because if I really made them understand how I feel it would make them feel the same way and that would be two people miserable instead of only one.

from MR

My dearest Otto,

The drawing room has been turned into a sort of common room full of typewriters and gramophones and we all gather there in the evening. Uncle Edward and Miss Coverley have their own rooms and sometimes emerge when the children want to play games. I am so glad Lawrence is coming home on Monday.

Gem's engagement to Silk Pyjamas has been broken off. I do not think it matters very much, but she is devastated for the time being. They have taken the iron railings from round the parks. It looks so nice without them, like an American town where one garden runs into another and people can wander where they like.

We went to a bazaar in aid of Russia the other day. Mrs Saunders raffled a pair of bedroom slippers made by herself. They made quite a lot of money. I got a pile of very thick oiled wool, which we are knitting into gloves for Russia. It is rather nice and smells like a threshing machine.

Ilse got a letter from her mother, the first for over a year. She and the children and the father are all right. I am so thankful. I was sure they had been killed. I cannot think how they got out of Holland.

Irene thought she had found a job at one of the big radio companies, but it fell through and she has been ploughing her way round labour exchanges. She has absolutely no clothes and even holes in her shoes as she has been living on 2/6 per week for the last six months. As she is only 18 she will not get anything with very much pay. It is horrid for her, poor child.

We are vaguely getting ready for Christmas. Last Christmas was one of the most ghastly things I can ever remember. The children are all very keen on it and none of the refugee girls has had a really proper one for years. I suppose it is right to do one's best.

With love from MR

DECEMBER 17, CHISWICK

My dearest Otto,

There is no doubt that you and another boy have had your papers lost or mixed up and we only discovered that by accident. It will take ages to put right, if such a thing can be done. Yes, you are right, we should be thankful that you arrived home all right. If you had been a few weeks later they would not have allowed you to travel[60]. It is so disappointing to find this internment business starting all over again and you waiting months in a camp while I rush round committees and write letters and sign papers and make a fuss.

Lawrence came home yesterday. We were able to take him to London to meet General de Gaulle. It was an interfaith conference at one of those lovely old halls in the City that are not open to the public, so we were lucky to see it. We had our names called out and shook hands with the hosts, including Bishop Henson [Bishop of Durham] in his scarlet robes, General de Gaulle and a little fat man whose name I never discovered[61]. General de G is a strange-looking man. His face is yellow and looks as if it were carved out of wood. He has a long straight nose and his hair is very black and sleekly plastered down. His tall, slim figure is the best part of him. Generally it is people's eyes or expressions that one notices first, but not with this man. There were a lot of important foreigners, the Bishop of London and the Chaplain General to the Canadian Forces. It was a wonderful gathering as it gave an idea of what the future might be like if all our political and racial differences could be forgotten in a great spiritual unity.

At the moment my only contribution towards reconstruction is to get you out. I don't mean I cannot do other things, but they are not any of them very constructive, just looking after my eight children and providing meals and doing housework, which takes up all my spare time and the not-spare time too. Even now Lawrence wants me to go for a walk. That is one reason why this letter is so weird, I am just rushing through it.

*continued next day*

---

60  On December 7, 1941, the Japanese bombed Pearl Harbor, an American naval base in Hawaii and the US entered the war.

61  The mystery man was most likely Gaston Palewski, de Gaulle's most trusted advisor and his liaison with the British Government. The lover of Nancy Mitford, he was portrayed in two of her novels as a French duke of immense charm.

This morning I went down to the WVS to sell certificates and stamps for war savings. I came back late for lunch, which has made everything late. It was nice and restful, as I sat down for a whole morning for the first time for two years.

I have a letter from Herbert, who has joined the Pioneers and is being put up in a hotel by the sea. His 'training' is learning to scrub floors and wash dishes, but he seems to enjoy it. He has also written to Ilse, which is rather amusing, as he always seemed to prefer Irene. However she 'ticked him off' badly just before he left because he was lazy about doing up his Christmas parcels and he has now swung round to the other side. Ilse is very beautiful, sweet and kind and that is all, nature having provided her with such a lovely outside the rest does not matter. Irene has not been given such a striking outside, but has rather too many brains and has not yet learnt that the best thing to do with brains is to hide them. There is good news – she has found work with the Girl Guides. I am relieved because she will be with nice people. I wish you could see both girls, I am so fond of them and it is lovely having them.

Have I told you about George, my newest refugee? He is from Vienna and was interned in Canada. He has turned out to be a connection of Mrs Saunders, a nephew of a cousin of hers. He is staying for a while before joining a munitions factory. He and Lawrence have been inside all day building one of those model aeroplanes. I must now go for another walk with Lawrence in the frightful cold. And then we have to go miles to St Paul's Cathedral to see a lot of children doing a nativity play.

With love from MR

My dearest Otto,

My mother had a tiresome accident and fell down stairs and bruised a bone on Christmas Eve. Fortunately she has help at home, so it was all right. She had to go to hospital but is out and well again now. Lawrence and Helen are going to stay with her a bit later on.

We are all well and had a lovely Christmas in spite of the war, because we had seven people in the house under 18, which is always fun. We had a turkey on Christmas Day and the Sisters from the cottage[62] came and brought a plum pudding and I bought one and I put things in them both, sixpenny bits and charms and all the children were very pleased when they got anything. It is rather a work of art sticking charms into puddings, but it was quite successful.

Helen has grown so pretty, tall and stately, with large eyes and she carries herself beautifully. Lawrence will be very nice-looking but at the moment seems to be mostly eyes and untidy hair. He is sweet and has such a lovely nature. The little girls are pretty and just at the point where they look a bit 'leggy', like puppies growing up. Well, I think I'd better stop.

With love from MR

---

62   The sisters of the Community of St Denys, an Anglican order, lived in a cottage next to the Vicarage and helped Edward with parish work.

*Sister Alethe brought a plum pudding for Christmas dinner.*

# 1942

**Otto has joined the Pioneers and is downhearted about the road building and other heavy labour undertaken by this auxiliary force in freezing conditions.**

JANUARY 1, CHISWICK

My dearest Otto,

I haven't heard from you in ages and hope you aren't too miserable. Have you ever tried standing mentally outside yourself to watch what is happening to you and other people? When you are very tired it helps you see more clearly. You can step into a peaceful place, which I should call the presence of God. It gives you a sort of power. You are no longer bogged down by 'things' and can get strength from a source of happiness inside yourself. If you can get through you can sometimes go right away to the most wonderful experiences. I suppose it is getting into another dimension. The easiest way is to be swept through by music, but one does not really need any outside help.

We have been having rather a hectic holiday. Helen has returned and gone to bed with a temperature. Yesterday I took eleven of the household to Kew for a picnic by the lake. It was very windy and we all went off at different times to shudder in the large palm house. I had to go home early to make the dinner and left most of the others going round the Wood Museum. No sooner had I arrived than the telephone rang and Miss Coverley said Anthea was lost! I knew she could not really be lost and gave instructions about telling men at the gates and suddenly there was a scream down the phone – Anthea was found again! She had been sighted by Gem and George, who were bicycling around looking for her.

On Monday most of them went to *Dumbo* and those who had seen *Snow White* were disappointed in it. As a work of art, I think *Pinocchio* is the best thing Disney has ever done, but the tunes of *Snow White* are better.

Fred Wright and Tasher are leaving and I shall have an empty room. I applied to have a Canadian to stay on leave, on condition they sent me one that did not mind Australians. In the end I gave up the idea as it did not even pay out-of-pocket expenses. One woman I heard of had two Australians and two Frenchmen and they had a great argument. The two Frenchmen went in hysterics to two different rooms and the Australians disappeared in a fury out of doors.

There is supposed to be a very good Penguin book on China. I heard it reviewed on the wireless and tried to find it on the bookstore but saw nothing but *What is Wrong with the Army, How to Grow Good Food, Murder by Madmen* and periodicals about the ARP and AFS [Auxiliary Fire Service].

With love from Aunt Molly

JANUARY 6, CHISWICK

My dearest Otto,

My fingers are frozen and covered with chilblains, which have burst and I think the typewriter is frozen too. Thank God the water is still running, but I expect it is merely a matter of hours before that goes as well.

This letter should have been posted yesterday, but I was too busy to write. Helen is packing her school trunk. At the last moment her gym tunic disappeared, but thank goodness turned up just in time.

Uncle Edward is interviewing replacements for Fred. He is considering a married curate with a young wife. I cannot cope with new curates and their wives. She will be pretty with big eyes, fluffy hair and a good complexion. She will wear her clothes as if she had thrown them on in the dark and will not put powder on her nose. She will have a soft voice and a bit of a Yorkshire accent. He will be tall, with a long face and big feet and look as if he has no insides. Very soon they will have a baby and I shall have to be very enthusiastic and produce baby clothes. I feel fed up, very tired and don't want to be excited about a baby or anything else.

A spark has just flown out of the fire and burnt Anthea's bodice. It will now need a patch as big as the garment.

Helen and I are talking of sliding down to Chiswick to buy a 'spread' for her to take back to school. I have no jam for her or Lawrence and they have to take something. The next-door clergyman's wife wants us all to go to tea with her today and I am going to be beastly and not go. Their name is Warren and the house is warren-ish too and always reminds me of a rabbit burrow. Actually she is nice, but I can't stand her just at present.

There is no letter from you today, but I know you are all right. I can't think of anything that could happen to you on the Isle of Man except death by boredom.

I am sorry to be so cross. I will try to write nicely tomorrow after I spend most of the day in the underground and in the biting cold of Turnpike Lane getting the children onto their buses back to school. I am not sure if I shall manage it. Also I have to get Lawrence some football boots and other last-moment things. Everyone is out and the house is so quiet and ghostly, like an empty shell. I must stop as otherwise the joint will not be ready for lunch.

With love from Aunt Molly

P.S. I have lost my pen.

JANUARY 18, CHISWICK

My dearest Otto,

A wave of crime is sweeping over Chiswick. It is rather like living in a detective story. The other night I was woken by a noise in the kitchen and called out because I thought the cat had knocked something down. Everything was quiet, but a few minutes later I heard another noise and saw a little light like the flame of a match. Then I shouted, "Who is there?" and hopped out of bed to find the kitchen blind was blowing because the window was open. I shut and bolted it and went back to bed. The next morning when I took down the blackout I found a great ladder put up outside the garden door. If I had not been sleeping downstairs in the study, he could have taken anything from the ground floor. Because it was so cold both dogs were sleeping upstairs.

Apparently a man had been told that the first house in the Mall was furnished and untenanted. He pinched a ladder from

Bedford House and tried our place, found he had made a mistake and went on to Mrs Radford at Woodroffe House. Then he went to the Herberts' at Hammersmith Terrace. The daughter Crystal was asleep with her husband, who was home on leave. His uniform coat was hanging on the bedpost and the thief went through all the pockets and took everything of value. Last night someone broke into the schoolroom behind the church, which is now a rest shelter and removed four pounds' worth of crockery. On the way home from work George met a policeman taking off a very fierce-looking man with a sack on his back and we wondered if it was full of items from the schoolroom. Irene goes all Russian on these occasions and wants to get bloodhounds going.

People are getting quite jumpy. Tom Nelson (next-door but two) now goes to bed each night with a knuckleduster by his side, two huge dogs at his door and a loaded revolver beneath his pillow. I do not know why he should think a burglar would attack him. I'm sure the last thing most thieves wish to do is to kill anyone. By the way, The Clarendon was fined £60 last week for selling 'black-market' goods. It is odd they should fine them a sum that is probably only half the takings for one evening. They should have taken three months' profits.

There is absolutely no other news as it is too cold for anything to happen.

With love from Aunt Molly

*Tom Nelson went to bed
fully armed after a rash
of robberies in the Mall.*

**Anticipating some leave in February, Otto writes to Molly to plan a visit to the Vicarage, the first since his arrest in June 1940.**

My dearest Otto,

I am so delighted and relieved to get your letter and read that you are coming home at last. I am keeping your week of leave as free as possible. It will be lovely.

I like that you write about the good things at camp: the rides on the lorry and the black lamb and the wild horses. I think that is how people's prayers are answered. If you pray for someone and do not know what to ask, the prayer is turned into something lovely that will help them. Perhaps the black lamb was one of your mother's prayers, all soft and gentle and lovely, come down from the heavens in that form.

I expect you will travel through Wednesday night on the 4th, arrive in London, have a hot shower and appear here at 11 am more or less sleepwalking and looking like a Christmas tree slung about with tin hats and other warlike equipment.

I meant to write before but have been so busy lately. The silly part is that there is nothing to show for it. I might as well have remained in bed all day.

Patience will be here on half term while you are here. This is a good thing as she announced that whatever part of the term it happened to be she was returning home, because all the other girls got off when their brothers had embarkation leave. I saw myself caught in a hopeless argument about it all with her teachers. Anyway let's hope and pray it is not embarkation leave you are having.

Next week Uncle Edward goes into hospital for his nose. My brother had that operation a few years ago. For ages his nose was so bad he could not blow it, then he had it fixed and he could not stop blowing for six months, after which time it settled down.

I have been rushing round looking at nursery schools in case Helen would like to work at one. I worry I am just making her do all the things that I would have done when I was her age if I had had the chance. On the other hand, when one is very young one needs people to advise one on what to do. There were about 15 small, fair-haired little creatures of 3 to 5 at the school I saw today. It is very sweet but there is always a noise going on and it is very restless, much worse than in a family setting where children are at different stages of development. I think that children should grow up in a family and not in a nursery school, but as there is no domestic help to be obtained now there is no choice. Anyway this discussion of nurseries is not very suitable material for a letter to a very young Pioneer, so I had better stop.

Looking forward so very much to Thursday week.

Love Aunt Molly

P.S. I have bought a pair of clogs. They have caused a sensation on the Mall.

*Molly in her clogs.*

**Otto's Pioneer company moves to Huyton, the camp near Liverpool from which he was sent to Australia.**

My dearest Otto,

Thank you so much for your letter, which arrived exactly on my birthday.

I must say it turns my blood cold to be writing to you at Huyton again. I wish you could have gone somewhere else. Yes, I know all about the waste of manpower. There is as much waste of womanpower (if there is such a word) and of other things. It makes me so angry I don't like thinking of it. There seems to be no excuse for the conditions being so bad – it is too silly and I am so awfully sorry.

The weather here is still icy and I expect it is worse where you are. I tried to get you a torch, but although they have plenty in the shops, they have no batteries. I wish I knew someone in Liverpool who would give you a bath when you want one. I sent you one pair of pants and hope they are right. I registered the parcel because Mrs Rae-Scott sent Philip six pairs of pants and six vests but her parcel never arrived. I think myself that Philip would have found such a lot of underwear an embarrassment and it was a good thing they did not turn up.

Teddy is at Amwell Bury recovering from his operation and spending time with the little girls. I go down for a couple of nights each week.

A burst pipe in the attic flooded down into the drawing room and it was all rather alarming. We have put buckets and sheets up there to stem the tide and the builder says he can do nothing till the snow has gone. Anyway now the water is frozen so it is no longer coming in. George mended the pipe by doing it up with a bicycle tyre inner tube.

I am sitting on the very edge of the big chair because Bonny has tucked himself in behind me and is trying to push me off. George went to bed some time ago and Irene has just gone and Ilse is finishing a letter to Herbert. This is very good for her English and must be encouraged. A letter written by Ilse usually has about six other people helping with it.

I will see you very soon.

Love Aunt Molly

**Otto has spent his leave at the Vicarage, returning for the first time in 18 months. Anthea recalls that Molly made sure it was a quiet week for Otto to talk, sleep, read, go for walks and enjoy civilian life.**

FEBRUARY 14, CHISWICK

My dearest Otto,

I was glad to get your lovely long letter as you sounded more settled and less miserable than before. Did I look worried when I saw you off? You'll have to get used to it because I am constantly crying when seeing Lawrence off to school although I know he is all right. It is merely selfishness. I hated your going and it did seem like nothing but cruelty to children pushing you off after only seven days when you should have had much longer to settle down to life again.

Yesterday I went to Peter Stadlen's Schubert concert[63]. He plays beautifully but I was frightfully tired and know so little about music. I made straight to the hot grid on the floor and sat on top of it. Remember we saw a little man sitting on it last time after we had been frozen in the front of the hall? I think one hears just as well from the back. Before the concert started, a magnificent person strode into the room. He was about 6' 3" with long hair and a full beard and side-whiskers. He wore a great golden cloak that swept from his shoulders to the ground. He certainly needed attention and he got it.

I am going to work in the British Restaurant[64] in Chiswick. They give excellent food and most of the help is free. Actually it would

---

63  Peter Stadlen, a Viennese composer and pianist, was, like Otto, arrested and sent aboard the *Dunera* to internment in Australia. He organised an orchestra and a 50-voice choir for his camp.

64  The Ministry of Food set up these non-profit canteens run by local committees. Meals were 9d, just over £1.50 in 2013.

be a very expensive way of feeding a family but works out cheaply for one or even two people who need a meal. It is supposed to save overhead expenses for people who are alone all day so they do not have to light fires and cook for themselves. Actually I think no one ever does this. If they are alone they may have bread or cheese or cocoa or something that does not need much or any cooking. However the government could not know that and the scheme must be needed as so many people come to be fed.

Last week Robin Hay[65] came back on leave from the Marines and Mrs Hay brought him to Sunday school. She was so pleased to show him off that her efficiency as a teacher evaporated 95 per cent. However Robin made up for it by taking all the boys in one class and teaching the lot. They were thrilled at having someone in uniform instructing them.

The husband of Gwen Owen, who had her wedding reception here, has been ordered abroad. She is feeling rather down, poor girl. Tropical kit[66].

We are having another prospective curate to see us on Tuesday. Would you like *The Spectator* by any chance? If you don't mind its being late it can be sent to you at the end of its round. It goes to two other people.

Everything is now on 'points' including rice and cocoa[67]. I feel we are coming in for a very bad time as far as this war is concerned.

With love from Aunt Molly

FEBRUARY 17, CHISWICK

My dearest Otto,

I started working at the British Restaurant on Monday. It was fun and really proper work, not just hanging about waiting for things

---

65  The Hay family lived in Kensington and came to church at St Nicholas. Their children, Robin and Heather, were popular with Molly's family.

66  'Tropical kit' meant a uniform and supplies for warm weather. It was likely the only advance information given to Gwen's husband, as troop movements were kept secret.

67  From December 1941, the rationing system included a monthly allowance of 16 discretionary points for a selection of foodstuffs.

to happen. I should imagine it is just like a NAAFI [Navy Army Air Force Institutes] canteen, but for civilians. We had about 500 people through in two hours. They get a ticket and collect their food from the hatch and later return the dirty plates, which are washed up by me and some other people. There is something Russian about it all – the people are so drab, dressed in dark clothes and most of them are very rough. The hatch frames them like a picture. The US civilian idea of a soldiers' canteen is hundreds of godlike young men, smart in their uniforms, collecting their rations with a smile and a salute for the pretty, plump ATS girls who, with every curl on duty and every lip well-sticked, present them with a steaming plate. Well, we are the other side of that picture. Ordinary, ugly civilians in very bad clothes (men, women and a lot of children) presenting a ticket and being fed and washed up for by a quantity of very thin and worried-looking elderly ladies with streaky hair and no lipstick. There was heaps of hot water and no messing about with kettles and I am very quick at that sort of thing so I think I was useful. I became really clean for the first time in ages.

On Sunday we had Philip Rae-Scott (home on leave) with Midge and their mother in for tea and played Monopoly afterwards. Miss Coverley and I had to join in to make up numbers and I found it frightfully dull as I could not pretend to be interested in getting and losing vast sums of money. The young people were supremely happy. I think perhaps life for them is so quick and exciting that they like something very slow and dull as a contrast.

Philip looks very nice in uniform. He has much improved and likes his work and looks very clean. This he should do, as he says he has a whole ounce of soap all to himself just for washing his body (not for clothes or scrubbing floors). I don't call it fair. I think if you do housework and make fires you should have a larger allowance than just a man by himself.

With love from Aunt Molly

P.S. I meant to enclose a programme from Peter Stadlen's Schubert concert, but it has got very crumpled. The girl who sat next to me, who came in with an airman she called "darling", so she must have been engaged to him, said that PS played the *allegro vivace* much too fast. Miss Hughes at the WVS, who was the head of a music school, says Schubert is frightfully difficult to play and so full of ideas he got simple effects by very complicated methods and unless a pianist has the 'feel' of Schubert, the pieces are very difficult. I wish you could have heard him, as you would have understood all about it.

FEBRUARY 20, CHISWICK

My dearest Otto,

There is still no letter from you, from which I conclude that everything is still ghastly. I will write anyway because if I don't get you and Helen posted on Friday, or Saturday latest, it is difficult to get letters off to family in Africa and America.

I had hoped it would be better for you when the weather broke. After enduring the great heat in Australia, you could not have had a worse beginning than the bitter cold of Liverpool. The weather here is at last improving, for the first time in weeks we are warm enough in bed to be able to sleep. Also we did not have any more burst pipes and the floods in the attic have died down. There only remains a tiny trickle of water.

Last week I went to see *Hatter's Castle*, a well-done, unpleasant film with a good moral. Afterwards there was a saucy American potboiler about catching spies in the USA. The cast was horrid but I liked a scene that showed a sleeping apartment of the American Marines. They all had sweet little beds with blankets, two sheets and a pillow in a lovely clean case. I think everyone should join the American Marines.

Today I drew my soap ration[68] for the month and have decided to become a brunette. It will be quite impossible to stay clean enough to remain blonde. Also I shall dye all my underclothes black. Mrs Porteous gets a little extra soap because her husband is a doctor[69].

---

68  From February 1942, the monthly soap allowance was a choice of 4 oz household soap or 2 oz toilet soap.

69  Mrs Porteous was married to R K Porteous, the Rich family doctor.

Presumably the government thinks that doctors should be clean.

Did you see that 60 million pounds had been quite literally 'sunk' in that Singapore Base[70]? Millions in cash and lives lost. Perhaps by the time this is all finished we will accept that most of the solid things one can see and feel, that take up so much space and so much time, are no good. They can't be worth anything because time and space do not exist and are only artificial standards by which we measure our existence here.

I saw five swans flying over the water yesterday morning. They were making that fascinating and unearthly sound that swans make. Like a lovely Japanese picture – only nowadays one says Chinese instead of Japanese. I'm afraid there are thousands of prisoners taken in Singapore. I am so thankful you are no longer behind barbed wire.

There are thousands of ducks on the river outside this house and people have been writing to *The Times* about it. They look like huge robins with red breasts and green-brown plumage. They live in Norway and in the winter usually fly to the north of Scotland for warmth. When it is very cold they are driven further south to England. They are permanent refugees.

The Croasdells rang up to tell me Myra Hess will be playing at the National Gallery[71]. I shall try to take Teddy, I think he would enjoy it. He is not very well and has rheumatism and feels very cold and rather miserable. It was a bad time of the year to have a nose operation.

Mrs Saunders is finally leaving Red Lion House and I went to help with packing up. She has a chair covered from the parachute of a shot-down airman. It is a very lovely, springy blue-green silk with a gold lining and bound with the blue cord held by the airman. I should not like to have it on one of my chairs somehow. I wonder what happened to its owner.

---

70   The UK surrendered Singapore Base, the centre of its Pacific defence, to the Japanese on February 15, 1942.

71   Pianist Myra Hess organised and often played lunchtime concerts at the National Gallery, which took place on weekdays from October 1939 until April 1946. The museum now hosts a Dame Myra Hess Day annually in October.

Helen wrote that she fell down half a flight of stone steps onto her nose. It rather horrified me, because she said she had a lump sticking out from it. I hope she hasn't broken it.

Don't forget to tell me if you want anything sent on. I am knitting another pair of socks your size. Will you manage to let us have a postcard soon, it does not matter about a letter.

Don't let things get you down or make you too unhappy. This is my second war so I know all about the mess and the mud and the horrid people one has to meet and the other unpleasant things. I think you have a great future before you. You will not be well-known or rich but that does not matter. You will do a lot to make people see things in the right way and having been through everything as you have and having hated it so much, will help you to help them. I know this does not seem possible to you now, but I know I am right.

With love from Aunt Molly

MARCH 1, CHISWICK

My dearest Otto,

I am wondering if you are all right, because I have not had a letter or postcard for ten days. Your Thursday letter did not arrive as usual on Friday. Are you walking about with it still in your pocket, by any chance? Have you been moved, or are you in hospital?

All the people round here have chills and coughs or rheumatism. We are getting colder and colder and I don't know how we shall manage with so little coal. We have unfortunately lent some of ours to people who have none. I know I shall never get it back. Irene and I are now sitting practically in the fire. I have half the grate filled up with a brick so as not to burn so much fuel, but it does not heat the room at all. Anyway, I suppose we should not grumble at being cold and dirty because if the Germans had invaded we would be freezing and filthy.

I expect you have seen that William Temple is to be the new Archbishop of Canterbury. There was rather a spot of bother about that because Churchill and his friends objected to Temple's Labour sympathies. Then he upset things by saying we should not cry out for vengeance but for justice and I think they were getting up a 'vengeance' campaign and he put a stop to it. He is supposed to have one of the largest brains in Europe, whatever that may mean. Once I was engaged to someone who was said to have the largest brain in Oxford, but he doesn't seem to have done anything very exciting with it. Rather disappointing.

Just now I am reading Daphne du Maurier's new book, *Frenchman's Creek*, which is disappointing. Lovely descriptions but so little story behind it.

I am having a couple to lunch today (sausages always for Sunday lunch, so the rationing is all right). I knew the young man – not so young now – as a baby in a pram when I was aged seven. He has been in submarines. Did I tell you all this before? It is so difficult writing to you five children and a brother and sisters each week – I can never remember what I told you all. He had a perfectly charming mother and when they were doing anything interesting at her house (for instance, painting the stable doors) she used to ask my sister and me to help. We also helped each year to make the hay. I still remember the smell of the hay and the glinting, flashing meadow brown butterflies, the smell of the sweet peas in the garden. It might be my imagination but the weather seemed so much warmer in those days, the shadows in the trees so much darker and thicker and the trees themselves cut so cleanly with their vivid green against the blue of the sky.

Mrs Saunders has let Red Lion House to our new curate. He is Mr Elmslie, a man of about 30. Mrs S is keeping some of her furniture there so as not to have to pay storage and, in exchange for the room it will take up, is giving the new tenant some fixtures, including the great mirror at the end of the sitting room, which of course she could not move herself.

With love from Aunt Molly

MARCH 5, CHISWICK

My dearest Otto,

Myra rang up last night to say she had heard from you, so you are all right. She says you are very cold in Huyton. The first thing my mother said when she heard you had gone there was, "What a dreadful place to send him – it is the worst climate in England".

It is very cold here too. The milk in the larder froze again and the washing is stiff on the line in the kitchen. It is the coldest year since the one before my husband was born. The ground is like iron again, too hard to dig, let alone to plant the most important vegetables.

The little girls are home for the weekend. I am being frightfully extravagant and am simply ladling on the coal for them. I have been freezing over a few embers for the last week, but intend for the next few hours while they are here to have the place warm. We will have to freeze again later on.

I took Patience to have her hair cut this morning and then we shopped a bit. I got a bundle of typing paper as I hear all paper is going out soon. Mrs Craig the postmistress says there are so few envelopes about, she usually orders a box at a time and now they will only send her a few packets. Did I tell you that Anthea is growing plaits? I think she will look very sweet. At the moment they are so short they look like thick little brushes sticking out of her head behind. She wants to have lovely long ones hanging over her shoulders.

The other day four privileged tickets arrived for a Russian ballet. My husband and I went to one performance and George and Miss Coverley to the other. It was very disappointing. I do not think ballet can be done successfully in wartime. To begin with the orchestra was made up of old men and girls. They might have been all right, but the first violin was a squeaker and spoiled the rest. For ballet one must have lovely costumes and they need constant renewing because the dancers get so hot. Well, all the costumes were *mauvais*, as the free Belgian soldier told his relations in the row behind us. Even from the dress circle they looked soiled. It must be impossible to get new clothes. One of the women was very good indeed. The solo man had a glorious figure and it was worth going from that point of view only. The chorus were the plainest I have ever seen, too plain even for the ATS. The first of the dances was called 'Red Star', with a dancer in Russian uniform and a lady dressed entirely in scarlet veils. Their clenched fists and STRONG GESTURES moved the tepid audience to clap.

We came out of the show halfway through and went to find a teashop that sold cakes. Cakes are not very nice and taste all alike, but at least they are sweet.

I imagine you have about a fortnight more at Huyton before leaving for Wales or Scotland. I should like to see you before you go. If I can fix up anything, could you get a few hours off? I want to see the two new cathedrals they are building. That is to say as well as seeing your silly face.

By the way the soap ration is not as bad as it seemed and somehow I have kept well to my allowance. Things like scrubbing the kitchen have come to an end. There is no soda now, either, which I am glad about. It has been so cold we have all had cracks on our fingers and thumbs and the soda at the canteen just finished mine off.

With love from Aunt Molly

P.S. If I am coming to see you it must be soon. Passenger trains are being taken off after Easter.

MARCH 22, CHISWICK

My dearest Otto,

Yes, there are often crossroads in life and we just have to make a choice with no guidance at all. I know how horrid everything must be for you. Still, I am sure you made the right decision in joining the Pioneers. There are men all over England sitting about in horrid conditions wasting their time. With a citizen army a certain waste of time is inevitable. There may come a time for you all when you will be needed very badly.

You know you would have been miserable thinking of Myra all alone in London if you were stuck in Australia and she on her part would have worried herself sick about you on the other side of the Japanese.

Did I ever tell you about our friend in the Hampstead Garden Suburb? She sat half a day for a whole year in an ambulance station at the beginning of the war. She grumbled about that waste of time and she was quite right. Then one night she had a call and the house she was sent to was her own. Since then she has continued sitting half a day at the ambulance station and nothing else has happened.

Poor little son, I am so sorry I can't be consoling or say anything to help. I hope you will be able to study, a great many men are learning in their spare time. Herbert writes that he is learning Spanish. You can study better on your own than with a lot of other people and perhaps you will be able to take up a correspondence course. You know that I hope you will write something one day.

Will you tell me what you think of my scheme to pop up to Liverpool? You may think the idea silly. You may say, politely, as you said when I suggested Myra go to the Isle of Man, "There is nothing I should dislike more than to see either of you here".

We are just going to take the children to Turnpike Lane. They will be back for Easter in three weeks, though Helen says they have scarlet fever, flu and pinkeye at her school, so they might not let them out.

With love from Aunt Molly

JUNE 24, NEWNHAM COLLEGE, CAMBRIDGE

My dearest Otto,

I am writing this out of doors on my knee and hope you will be able to read it.

Teddy and I left home on Monday to visit my mother and the little girls, who have left Amwell Bury now that the cottage renovations are done. They are very happy at Tollgate. It was an awful effort getting away from the Vicarage: scrubbing the kitchen, getting in rations and arranging for people's entertainment in my absence. We had a party at the cottage the first evening. It was a great success apart from the midges that made raids upon the guests. I was nearly eaten up. All Anthea's guinea pigs have been eaten by a dog. Patience is making quite a lot of money buying young rabbits at 1/6 or 2/-, feeding them for six weeks and selling them at 1/- per lb. Most rabbits run to 3½ lbs.

Everyone is depressed about the news from Africa[72], especially

---

72  On June 21, 1942, German forces took the strategic port of Tobruk in Libya, capturing 25,000 Allied troops.

because so many of our family are out there and we all know the North Coast where they are fighting. There seems nowhere to make a stand.

We spent two nights with my mother and came on to Newnham for an interfaith conference[73]. I left my umbrella and gas mask somewhere on the way. Newnham is a women's college just out of Cambridge, a big place with swimming pools and tennis courts and libraries and everything else you like. I wish I could send you here. The gardens are full of syringa trees, which are covered with wonderful white scented flowers. It is also full of dugouts from the last war. I suppose if there is a raid the conference will have to rush into them in its night attire. It would be a bother and I hope we will not get one.

It is lovely and warm and we all 'assemble for tea' at 4.30. I have not been to a conference before and did not think I should like it, but it seemed the only way of getting Teddy away for a holiday. Also I thought I might get some practical ideas about what is to be done with you and the others after the war.

The planes fly very low, just over our heads and make a great noise. One passed so close I could not hear myself write. I have just seen some of the conference arriving. They are all wearing hats and stockings, which means I must, too, I suppose.

With love from Aunt Molly

P.S. Did I tell you Hans turned up on Friday? He spent 10 days with us last summer holidays. I am glad he came back to see us. He is always very sweet to Teddy and me but with others seems to be very quarrelsome, constantly having rows. I think it must be the German element. If he were more Jewish, the fierceness would be neutralised. Is this possible? Anyway I hope Hans will spend some of his summer with us. He and Irene loathe each other, which is a pity, but they both must learn to get on with people they don't naturally take to and it is good for them meeting.

---

73   Leaders of the Church of England, the Roman Catholic Church and British free churches set out joint plans for the social regeneration of England.

**No letters from the summer of 1942 have survived. Hans is now studying in London and living at the Vicarage. Otto is preparing to move from a camp near Peterborough. Over the next 22 months, Otto will move frequently with the Pioneers throughout England and Wales and visit the Vicarage on leave as often as possible.**

NOVEMBER 8, CHISWICK

My dearest Otto,

Unless you hear to the contrary, I am expecting you on Friday next sometime after 11.00 am. I have changed my Restaurant day so will be in. I still don't see why you can't get ten days' leave. It is so much more of a rest and feels so much longer than seven. Did I tell you that Herbert has gone to a village near Marlborough and is billeted in a racing stable? Not very comfortable, I should think. I'm hoping to get him some introductions round there so he will have somewhere to go on his afternoons off.

There is no news. The other day I took two hours off to read the poems of W B Yeats. His poems are lovely but need taking in small doses. I think this is true of all poems. After all, people only write poems because they must. There is no economic reason because it seldom pays. They write because something inside them makes them do so and one gets a glimpse right down to their thought life. Yeats's mind is like a lovely dark etching with bits of bright colour in oil among the darkness. Have you ever thought how odd it is that a great many people may do the same thing every day, but their inner lives are different because they all think differently about the same thing. When you read a lot of one man's poems, you have in a small measure entered inside him. Well, this lecture on poets will now be terminated. Anyway you need not read it. That is the best part of letters – you can always skip and nobody minds because they don't know.

Gem is home on three weeks' holiday and immersed in a great many tea parties. We had a coffee party the other day that was a great success mainly due to the lovely fire created by the logs you sent. It was the first wood fire many people had seen this year.

Something really seems to be happening at last in North Africa[74] that I hope will clear the ground for the Russians. Some people think that North Africa is to be the 'second front'. I still think it might be Norway. Everyone has their own pet theory. Unfortunately most people want to start the second front in the country that appeals most to their affections. Some are keen on starting it in Italy or the south of France. Actually I wish it could be North Africa because that country is so sparsely populated there will not be so many civilians who will suffer.

It seems clear that people do dreadful things to each other even when everything is so lovely all around. They are beastly when there are silver and gold poplar leaves all moving in the rhythm of the wind and a carpet of gold under the trees in the forests and pine trees like etchings on blue sky and white clouds. I suppose if one could get inside a tired soldier's mind one would find he did not see any of these things. He might really be blind and it is not so much his fault as his misfortune.

A family called the Heatons,[75] Neville and Cecily, have replaced the Dutch people at The Hollies. Cecily just had a baby – it is another boy. We have all been suggesting exotic names like Wolfgang, Dominic, Siegfried and Lothar. She and Neville were expecting a girl, so did not bother thinking about boys' names. I'm afraid they are rather disappointed. Anyway boys are much easier to bring up than girls and are in most ways more satisfactory. Girls are frightfully difficult and you never know where you are with them. The big thing against having boys in the past was that they were so often killed in wars, at least in England, but now in most countries, the bombing makes war as dangerous for girls as for boys and just as horrible.

Well there is no news and Bonny is barking to be let in and I am hoping to see you quite soon.

With love from Aunt Molly

---

74  The Allied victory at the 2nd battle of Alamein was a turning point in the war.

75  Neville Heaton, a senior civil servant, led the team that put through the 1944 Butler Education Act, which set policy for the next four decades.

**Molly's mother dies of pneumonia on December 6, never having recovered from the death of her son Dick. Molly spends the following week at Tollgate with the little girls clearing the house. Deeply saddened by her mother's death, ill and exhausted, Molly spends a week in bed. She uses the time to thank friends for their letters.**

DECEMBER 17, TOLLGATE, AMWELL

My dearest Otto,

Thank you so much for two letters. I am awfully glad you have left that awful place at Peterborough. Even bad billets will be better than a camp. Also I am thankful you are having more or less normal work instead of the slave work you have been doing for the last year.

This is Sunday and I return on Monday. The little girls are here and it has been lovely having them. We all have our bicycles with us and rucksacks that the Heatons lent us. I am very glad we brought the bicycles because otherwise it is impossible even to get to the shops except by bus and one has to wait such a long time for them and they rarely go to the right places.

I have spent hours and hours clearing things up and putting away and tearing up papers. I have almost finished now. The Amwell Bury woods are looking so lovely, with the trees all bare and like lace against the sky and in places the ground is covered with snowdrops.

There is nothing much to say. I think I shall have to send Anthea to The Barn School[76] in Much Hadham with Patience. It is rather difficult. Patience seems very happy, which is satisfactory. She has made friends with the other children. The only pity was they thought she was 13 instead of 11 and put her in too high a class and then put her down too low and generally made a muddle of it.

Looking forward to seeing you soon.

Love from Aunt Molly.

---

76   The Barn School was chaotic in the 40s, but Anthea was taught art by Irina Moore, the wife of the artist and sculptor, Henry Moore.

My very dear little son,

This is not a proper letter, but just to wish you 'Peace and Goodwill' this Christmas.

I don't think you will be able to come home for your 36 hours leave, so will you please go to a dance instead. I hope you will write soon. I am so afraid you are very unhappy and perhaps ill.

I wish you were here but that is just silly. When I went to Liverpool Street today the station was full of unhappy-looking young men, some with girlfriends or wives or mothers, all returning to their camps for Christmas. On the bus coming home I sat next to a lucky fellow who was coming back for Christmas leave, but he said he had not had any for four months.

With love from Aunt Molly

# 1943

**The letters for 1943 begin in March. Otto has been at the
Vicarage on leave. After nine years at St Nicholas, Edward is
looking for a new parish.**

My dearest Otto,

There is nothing to tell you, so this will be a very short letter. I
hope you got back all right. It was lovely having you home again
and in the end I did not mind your going quite as much as before,
because you seemed less tired and more able to cope with things.

I think what you said the other day about people not being grateful
enough for what they have is so true. I met someone who has a son
in the Air Force and a daughter in the WRENS. She is a Red Cross
nurse and I asked what she did when they came home on leave. She
replied that she could not give up her work to be with the children,
but that they were out all day and did not mind if she was in or not
"as long as they had a good meal and a bed". She sounded rather sad
about it and I thought how lucky I was that all you children are so
sweet to me, from you down to Anthea and never make me feel as
if you don't mind if I am there or not. Resolved: to turn over a new
leaf and be grateful.

After you left I scrubbed and washed everything in sight, from
the kitchen floor to all the clothes[77]. Now I have landed myself deep
in the committee meetings that I refused to attend when you and
the children were home. I have been asked to address a women's
prayer meeting in Hammersmith, which I don't want to do, but it
is inevitable. I am a bit terrified as they are all Nonconformists. I
can usually get anything I want across to women and I suppose the

---

77    After the Chiswick Laundry was bombed in September 1940, Molly washed all the
      household clothes in the Vicarage bathtub.

psychology of a Nonconformist cannot be very different to that of a C of E churchwoman, except they are more fundamental. I suppose it will be all right.

The last *Country Life* had some rather nice pictures and an article by Christopher Hussey on housing[78]. It does not amount to much, as he himself says, but I liked the plans of the towns and villages: 5000 inhabitants, five shops and a nursery school as a unit and for five of these a church and secondary schools. I was surprised to find they did not consider a picture-house necessary till there is an even larger group of people to cater for.

Mrs Volkov has three medical students boarding with her. Last night she was away and they came home dead drunk and left all the lights on without putting up the blackout. At 12.15 wardens and police had all congregated outside the house and had to break their way in to turn out the lights. Nothing would wake the boys, not even slapping their faces with wet towels. Several police remained by their beds waiting for a 'statement' when they woke. I can't think what it would feel like to wake with a very thick head and a couple of policemen by your bed. It is a good thing for the boys because it will give them a fright and they won't get drunk again in a hurry.

I'm sorry your shoes are such a long time being mended, but you had worn them through at the heels and toes to the last rung of leather and another wearing would have made a hole through. They will be ready for you on your next visit.

With love from Aunt Molly

APRIL 16, CHISWICK

My dearest Otto,

I wonder how you are getting on and if you have moved to join a company. It does make such a difference to have nice people with one. I rang Myra up yesterday and a very fierce voice answered

---

78    Molly is referring to "Cities of the Future: The 'Rebuilding Britain' Exhibition at the National Gallery" by Christopher Hussey, published in the February 26, 1943 issue of *Country Life*.

the phone stating the name of the firm. When I asked for "Miss Walker"[79] the voice got quite human and nice. I thought it would have been a better advertisement for the firm if the phone had been answered by a mild voice in the first place.

There is nothing much to tell you. George is in lodgings now with a woman with the rather warlike name of Mrs Carrot. We have new rabbits that are getting on very well. George came over on Saturday and we went round to the Heatons and brought back a hutch with us. The Heatons have purchased 18 day-old cockerels for a few pence each and nine have died. One has to be prepared for a good many deaths, but it is worthwhile bringing up the rest.

Yesterday Irene came in with a face like a plum pudding, all covered with red spots. She had been sent back from the Girl Guides office with a temperature, but instead of coming home she had gone to a cinema, which seemed rather antisocial, especially for someone who hopes to do relief work in Europe after the war and should have a well-developed social conscience. I insisted on her going to the doctor because it looked like German measles and next week I shall have nine people in the house all under 21. She is still very cross with me, but thank goodness it is only a food rash. Hans has exams next month, so we would have been in a mess if it really had been measles.

With love from Aunt Molly


APRIL 27, CHISWICK

My dearest Otto,

This is not a proper letter but I have cut my finger and cannot type until the end of the week. There is not a lot to say, but even if there were, you would not be able to read it in this scribble, so perhaps it is just as well.

We had a very hectic Easter Monday, with 14 for lunch and 18 for tea and the cups and saucers ran out. As it was so cold we played games in the afternoon and some of the children went to the church

---

79   Like Myra, many refugees with German surnames used an English name at work.

tower, which is always a good form of entertainment. I have done nothing for the last six days but produce large amounts of food. We had boiled eggs for breakfast on Easter Sunday – at least some of us did, there were not enough to go around – and Patience painted them with watercolours. We also hogged up the chocolate you sent.

The church looked very lovely with masses of lilies. There are so many flowers out now, all at the same time. In Kent the farmers say they will be picking cherries in May. This has not happened for about 100 years.

I have decided to have Anthea home for the autumn term and send her to Colet, the junior school for St Paul's at Hammersmith. She will go with two girls who live nearby, Rachel Austin and Mary Townsend. There seem to be so many difficulties about rations and anyway she has to have a peculiar gland in her neck seen to and I'm afraid it will mean the hospital for a couple of days. I went to see Miss Wigg, the High Mistress of St Paul's, on Monday. She is charming. I told her Anthea was bad at maths and she said all the years she had been teaching she had never taught a generation that had so little idea about maths before, that they could not even learn their tables. I said I thought it a psychological reaction to all the mechanical devices by which the children are surrounded and she said she thought it was because they cannot concentrate.

I am taking Helen to have her eyes tested today. She says the blackboard at school is a mere blur to her, which is why she failed to pass an exam. I don't really think this statement is correct. Hans is passing another exam in July and after that he is keen to enlist in the Royal Engineers. He can do that now without going into the Pioneers first. A few of the children look to be coming down with flu.

I'm hoping there will be a letter from you in the next post.

With love from Aunt Molly

MAY 4, CHISWICK

My dearest Otto,

I am busy getting things ready to put into trunks. No, you have been wrong thinking of me 'rushing upstairs with trays' because the people who were ill this holiday needed no trays. Helen told Hans his fortune and said he was to be ill and taken away in an ambulance. He has been steeling himself ever since to being removed in this manner and even came to me one day and gravely suggested it might be as well to find out how one ordered ambulances so as to be in readiness.

Herbert writes that he thinks he has got into the paratroops. He went up for an interview and said they were very pleased to hear he was such a good shot (he'd won a prize for shooting) and also that he spoke Latin. We cannot think why Latin should have interested them.

Perhaps you are right about everyone having certain experiences they have to go through. I suppose there is a rough outline that every life has to follow up to a certain point and it is this outlining of predestination that some people can discern if clever at telling 'fortunes'. I think you have had two great experiences already in this war and will probably have a third and the best thing is for you to wait and get ready for it when it comes.

I am arranging to go away in July to Staffordshire with Teddy to stay with his sister, but I'm also arranging so that if you get leave I can return. Anyway I shall not be away for more than 10 days because of leaving Anthea and the rabbits, all of whom will have to be parked out.

Uncle Edward has just been offered yet another job, this time in Newcastle. They get further and further north, the next will be in the Isle of Skye or Iceland I think. We are unlikely to go to Newcastle as it is a devastated area and there are no houses. Even if there were we could not house-hunt from Chiswick. Also it is a very small salary and most of the first year's income would be taken up in the move. I do not think it would be a nice place to go to. If you're a southerner, it is no good going up north when you are middle-aged. There is about the same difference in temperament that there is between Prussians and the Viennese. The southerners madden the northerners because of their untidiness and dirtiness and general lack of thriftiness and the northerners are incomprehensible to the southerners who cannot get behind their forthright exteriors.

I should not mind that part because I understand people, but the others would not like it. I think it downright silly to offer a married man a job with a very small salary and no house. Even if we did go we would be here for your next leave and these days two months is the furthest one can look ahead.

With love from Aunt Molly

MAY 7, CHISWICK

My dearest Otto,

What do you think of this Russian/Polish business[80]? I think the Russians murdered the officers, because they murdered most of the upper-class people in the countries they went into. After all, one has to expect that because theirs is a class war. I also imagine they left all the identity papers in a dump and the Germans knew all this and found the papers months ago and were all ready to produce the story at a critical moment. It is incredible how men and women can think in their dealings with their fellow men.

I have just jammed a fork into my bad finger again, so I'm almost learning to use all my hand instead of two fingers only.

The chestnut tree is out and the flowers look almost exotic against the very dark green. I have been watching a thrush building a nest very high up at the top of the tree. The green is already almost as dark as in summer. My little peas are coming up and we had spinach from the garden last week.

I think Herbert must be working very hard at his paratrooping because he has sent home all his civilian shoes in a sack. He did love dancing so much. No more dancing! Poor Herbert.

It is pouring with rain and we're going out to tea, so I had better stop.

With love from Aunt Molly

---

80   On April 13, 1943, Germany broadcast news of a mass grave of over 4,000 Polish officers in Katyn Forest, near the Russian city of Smolensk. All were prisoners of war executed by Soviet secret police in 1940.

My dearest Otto,

If you have been given someone else's leave by mistake it is just too bad for the other chap. I really can't get up any great enthusiastic sorrow about it. There are such a lot of things I want to ask you but they can all wait.

Herbert came back on leave very suddenly on Thursday. He has done his training, which should have been eight jumps but was cut down to four jumps. Two jumps from a balloon, 70 feet high (the height of a barrage balloon) and two from a plane. They are not really 'jumps' – you sit on the edge of a hole with your legs dangling in space and look up towards a light. When it shows red you get ready and when green you push yourself off into space. Your equipment comes down also by parachute. I think it sounds horrid, but Herbert does not mind it. He is in the 21st Independent Parachute Company, which is handpicked and composed of all nationalities: English, Poles, Germans etc. You have to have a certain standard of education and intelligence before being allowed in because in the beginning they found all the paratroops were frightfully tough but had no brains. I suppose it is an honour that Herbert should have been chosen, but it is rather miserable all the same. Anyway he is very pleased with his maroon beret and with all the things on his sleeves and as there are only a few stray girls and myself to mind what happens to Herbert it does not matter so much. I am very much afraid he will go overseas now.

Ilse has had her calling-up notice and goes for an interview on Friday. I hope she will be sent somewhere, because the hat business is rather a dead end and she would be much happier in a hospital where she would meet new people. She makes friends easily but has got into a dull little set. It is time she pushed off into something wider.

Hans is still revising for his exams, immersed in enormous drawings and plans all over the floor of his bedroom. George came here for tea today. He saw Myra at church in the morning and recognised her because I'd lent her the earrings he had made for me. Unfortunately he is rather miserable, working 10-hour days and fire-watching at nights and he may have to move house. He is thinking of giving up munitions and joining the Royal Engineers.

They now allow us to go just once to the food office for ration books even if we have a lot of different names in our house. I'm very glad about it because I saw myself standing for all your leave in a ration-book queue at the library. One has to wait for hours and hours and the best thing to do is to take a book and knitting and make a day of it.

We are having such lovely weather. We had tea today under the fig trees after Sunday school, with George and the Hays and in the end Cecily blew in with some rabbit food and it was really nice.

With love from Aunt Molly

JULY 22, CHISWICK

My dearest Otto,

I've had a letter from you yesterday and no sooner had I digested it than Patience rang up announcing her intention of returning from school next day instead of after the weekend. Also all the new ration books had to be stamped and trains and ration books and marquees and very heavy suitcases seemed to run into each other all through the day.

In the evening I rang up to settle all the details about Helen's coaching for the School Certificate. We'd hoped she could be instructed privately with another child in the Mall, but it was no good and we had to think of something else. Teddy rushed up to town to see if the Poly gave Cert. coaching. They do not, so we wired to a school Cecily Heaton told us about where they did once say they would take her. We are waiting for the answer now. Irene is preparing for her Ranger test for the Guides. Meanwhile the Newtons (the people next door to the Heatons) and Ilse's cousin Brendt have both had baby girls. We heard about Brendt's baby during lunch – they rang up to tell Ilse.

Oh yes, Anthea has seen a specialist about the gland in her neck, which pops up under her chin whenever she eats a tart apple. We ended up in Richmond during an astonishing cloudburst. We couldn't find where the specialist had his consulting rooms and waded in our soaked cotton frocks and shoes past tall and beautiful houses on Richmond Hill. In the end in desperation I stopped a tall man running under his umbrella and asked if he knew the address we were looking for. He invited us into his house, which was so lovely, full of shining floors and ticking clocks. And he found the address in the telephone book and directed us to it. Before we left, I made little hats for Anthea and myself by knotting the four corners of our handkerchiefs, but of course it did little to stop the rain. Finally and rather late, we arrived at the specialist. Anthea sat and ate a green apple she had in her pocket and the gland obligingly popped up. It seems there is nothing that can be done, but as it is not harmful in any way, she will simply have to live with it.

Miss Coverley is going away for a real holiday on Monday. The last time she left home she was looking after her brother and nephews all the time and had no rest.

With love from Aunt Molly

P.S. They cannot take Helen at the school Cecily suggested.

JULY 29, CHISWICK

My dearest Otto,

A great many things have happened lately. George turned up on Sunday having at last made up his mind. He has joined the Air Force where he's going in a bomber crew and hopes to be on wireless. He stayed for tea. Afterwards Ilse and I went to Hertfordshire, where I left her at the rest home at Amwell Bury for a holiday. She was looking rather forlorn, poor little girl, but I think she will enjoy a week in the country. It will be nice for her to see how English country people other than town dwellers live. She was a bit horrified to hear there were no shops within a radius of a mile, but cheered up a bit when she saw some cows in a field.

Lawrence is home. He has grown two inches and looks very well and is full of beans. Helen comes tomorrow. We have decided on a school for her next term, St Felix,[81] but I am awfully afraid she will

---

81   St Felix had evacuated from Suffolk to Hinton St George in Somerset.

not like the idea of starting another school. It is supposed to be the best school in England, so I hope it will be all right.

Anthea has made enormous friends with Rachel Austin next door, which is a good thing as they will go to school together in the autumn term. They will be joining a convoy to Colet setting out from the Townsend's house every morning at 8.30.

I have been teaching Anthea geography. She knows nothing at all and Rachel knows nearly nothing. I think it is the way they are taught. Instead of learning facts about the world and looking at places on maps, they learn about latitudes and longitudes and the things made at various places. All this is necessary, but I am sure one should first know small things like the shape of the world and where the equator is.

With love from Aunt Molly

*Ilse was horrified to hear that there were hardly any nearby shops in the country, but cheered up when she saw a cow.*

My dearest Otto,

Hope you are all right in Wales and not too hot. Yesterday the children spent most of the time in the swimming baths. At the hottest part of the day they saw a lot of soldiers in full kit marching with packs. Awful. Irene arrived home from work like a drowned rat having been caught in a great thunderstorm that blew up on a very strong hot wind after supper.

The Bishop of Newcastle has discovered that there are no homes to be had in the city, so the offer of that job for Uncle Edward is temporarily off.

Will you try for a transfer to the Army? The war with Italy may be more or less over, but Germany and after that Japan, must be dealt with and it may mean the people who are now in the Army must remain for another three years. I wish you could get a training of some sort, something you could build up on after the war. The chief thing is that the road building and brick-piling of the Pioneers are not very suitable occupations for you.

Everything is rather hectic now. The children are all passing, or trying to pass, or hoping to pass some sort of examination and the house is full of books on various subjects. I rushed through botany for Helen and then they said she would need zoology instead, so we got books on the subject from the library and in the end she needed biology, which is a fusion of all three. I seem to have acquired a varied and disjointed knowledge of one-celled plants and animals. It is very interesting, but I don't know if it is any good and after all it is Helen who has to pass the silly examination, not me. Then Patience announced that she was very backwards with grammar. The statement was borne out by a casual survey of her school report. We now do grammar each evening and she is getting on. Cecily Heaton produced a very good book lent her by a high-up official on the Board of Education[82].

On Monday Helen and I did a lunch-hour concert and then went to look for school books at Foyles. We came away with a first-steps

---

82    The official is Cecily's husband, Neville.

botany book. Helen's education is most odd. She knows quite a lot about things like photosynthesis and osmosis and nothing about petals and roots.

I hope you did not get the thunderstorm we had last night. Perhaps it was local, as we did not have the one you mention.

I have made a lot of plum jam. It is very nice.

I heard from Ilse, who is enjoying her holiday at Amwell Bury. I am rather relieved, as it is so different to anything she has ever done before I wondered if she would be very bored.

Irene has passed all her Guide tests and is very pleased with herself. There were a lot of wild slum children at her camp. They were very sweet but also lazy and naughty and two had to be sent home because they incited the rest of the children to mutiny. One day the Company went into the town and found one small girl had been going round the local Woolworths just lifting things from the counters when no one was looking. She honestly did not know it was wrong, but thought it the natural and proper thing to do.

Herbert has gone abroad and wrote from the boat. He mentioned seagulls. I should think he is going to North Africa.

Tomorrow they are having sports in Chiswick House grounds and all my family are entering for races. I asked Hans if he would do so, but he was slightly horrified at the idea. Why are students so grand on one side of themselves and so very unorthodox on the other? I think it is because they are too young to do anything on their own. Hans would do the silliest thing with other students at the Poly, because it is doing something in a crowd, but they none of them will do anything on their own.

Helen sends her love.

With love from Aunt Molly

DECEMBER 10, CHISWICK

My dearest Otto,

I am writing this in the drawing room. The time is 2 pm and the light is full on. Outside there is a good old yellow fog. Gem has retired to bed after being semi-up for two nights running. Ilse went to work this morning all lopsided with inflamed glands down her neck. My husband has just announced his intention of having flu.

There has been a certain amount of mild excitement because Irene has made friends with a young Pole who is getting her to teach him English. He is one of the people rescued by us from the Russians. He was an airman and was brought down over Russia. When they took him prisoner, they put him in a cell with nothing on but his shirt and turned a 300-watt electric light on his eyes. They left him there for 10 days then put him in a dungeon where it was completely dark. As a result his sight went completely. It has come back a bit now, enough for him to do engineering, but not enough for him to be an airman. So much for 'Our Fighting Friends'.

Bonny has had a funny lump on his leg for a long time. Yesterday it burst. It was a blood blister and so bled all over everything. I bound him up, put him under my arm and bicycled him to the vet where they did him up for the time being. I am afraid he will have to be operated on to have it removed. I know he should be put to sleep, but I just don't know how we would get on without him. I suddenly realised rather an awful thing yesterday. Out of the six members of our family serving (I mean close members, not cousins) three have been killed: my brother, Nancy's husband and Teddy's nephew. That is to say half the young men of the family have died. I suppose people with larger families are even worse off. Somehow the war has been going on for so long I never took in what was happening. You and Ralph and Teddy's brother are only alive I think because of your geographical positions. The other three went from the Army, the Navy and the Air Force.

I heard from Ralph the other day. He is doing a course in Kenya and on his way there he picked up an old *East African Standard* (the local rag of Kenya) and saw announced the remarriage of our sister Nancy. I am very glad and think it is the best thing she could have done.

We went to see Oscar Wilde's *Perfect Husband* yesterday [Molly means *An Ideal Husband*]. It is a four-act play that might have been very good (never excellent) if it had been compressed into three acts. The audience was amusing. It consisted of a great many very highbrow young people and a good many rather debauched older people (i.e. contemporary with the play). Middle age was represented by Teddy and me. There was also one Pioneer with a friend (his twin brother I think), one RE [Royal Engineer] with his mother and one stray soldier. That's all. It is curious to think of the lives led by the so-called 'upper classes' in the days of Oscar Wilde. I remember when I was a child going to old-fashioned houses which were furnished very much like the scenes in the play.

You have said no more about leave. I wonder if you are getting a transfer. It seems a long time since you came home for 36 hours. There is no *Listener* this week, – someone has pinched my copy. Excuse the smudges, they are glue.

With love from Aunt Molly

**Otto has been at the Vicarage on leave.**

DECEMBER 23, CHISWICK

My dearest Otto,

Lawrence has come home all right and has grown inches and needs an entire new set of clothes. I don't know what I will do about coupons. And he has got his Second XV rugby football colours. It was very much the last moment, so he certainly could do no harm to the Second XV by having them, but I'm glad he got them all the same. I cannot help thinking it was more his charm than his football that produced the colours.

With love from Aunt Molly

DECEMBER 26, CHISWICK

My dearest Otto,

I hope you got back all right the other day. There were awful accounts in the evening papers of the crushes at the stations, especially at Waterloo, where one queue was so long no one could find the end of it. I am very glad you had your leave when you did. The paper says that the invasion of Europe is now a matter of weeks, so I suppose this will be your last break. Last night on the wireless they predicted nine weeks, which would bring it to the beginning of March. Today's paper made the invasion appear imminent. Also it is so difficult to get about over Christmas. There are no buses and only very few trains.

On Christmas Eve Devonshire Road got very excited, slightly tipsy and very noisy. There was one particularly happy party outside the Three Feathers where people were playing mouth organs and singing and having drinks. They looked so friendly, I nearly joined them. However evidently the excitement did not agree with the inhabitants of the road, because next day and today (Boxing Day) it is like a street of the dead and I expect everyone is sleeping through their hangovers.

Lawrence and I went to London to get him a coat. It is a very nice one and he is very good-looking in it. We also bought a belt because I discovered that he had his trousers held up with a piece of rope. We saw some very bright silk ties in the shop and I asked the man serving about them. He said they were Italian ties taken off an Italian ship captured in the Mediterranean on its way to South America. I went to London again in the afternoon with Helen to buy tickets for *The Lisbon Story* [a musical spy drama at the Hippodrome]. They would not book anything under 15/- over the phone. We got two tickets all right.

Yesterday George, who has a nice long leave, came in to tea and brought a lovely cake. He also brought me a brooch he had made. It is awfully clever – a little gold fly with ruby eyes and a green body. After tea we went to the Heatons and stayed for supper. We played charades and it was really great fun. Hans would not come because when we asked him he had a grand fit and said it would be out of place for him to play games. When we all swept out on Christmas night taking George, he was sorry but of course his pride prevented him from changing his mind. I was sorry too because he does enjoy a party so much if he can forget he has to be 'that HANDSOME and INTERESTING-LOOKING young REFUGEE'. I think it is very good for him to enjoy himself and not good always to be the H and IR.

Tomorrow the Heatons come to lunch. I have discovered that we will be 15 at table and there is very little to feed them on as we were 12 on Christmas Day and ate most of the turkey then.

We had a very tiresome and silly time the night you left. Mr Owen [the Fire Warden] suddenly looked in while we were having supper and said there was a fire practice and would we be there at 8. Teddy and I swallowed our food and arrived on the dot. Of course no one else was there. Then Mr Owen and Mr Elwell turned up and Mr Elmslie, annoyed at being snatched away from his coffee and some of the Nelson party who had been called away just as they were starting their evening meal. We waited about for half an hour, then were given some forms which had to be filled in (in the dark) to say what house was on fire (for us it was Said House) and sent to the chief fire-watcher at the brewery, who was supposed to fill up another form and send it by messenger to the fire station on the High Road. Well, we did that and waited for half an hour, by which time we thought our fire would be well away, so sent another message. Half an hour later still some fire engines turned up but refused to have anything to do with us as they had turned out for a message from the Standard Yeast factory (also on practice). I overheard one fireman say there were ten engines going to the yeast factory and that there would be none left for us. This depressed us a lot, as we really felt Said House was now past any fireman's aid. Also Mr Elmslie still hankered after his coffee and I had some washing to do and the Nelsons wanted their supper and we had all been standing around for an hour and a half. In the end we gave up and returned home and late into the night we heard the Auxiliary Fire Brigade motors rushing down the Mall enjoying themselves very much, but much too late to save any part of the street from the ravages of the flames.

We all got quite a lot of presents this year in spite of the war. I gave all the children money as I could think of nothing else. I had said I needed ink and postcards, so now have enough ink to bathe in and enough postcards to build a house with. Lawrence and Anthea 'decorated' the house with ivy. It is very dark and sombre and makes us feel as if we were living in a grave. Even the lavatory is decorated with ivy growing up the chain. And there are two large trees of it in the bathroom.

I wonder what you did for Christmas Day, or did you just sleep through it?

With love from Aunt Molly

# 1944

My dearest Otto,

We had a very good gathering here for the New Year. For lunch we had the Heaton's Christmas present of one chicken and one hen and afterwards I boiled the remains for soup, which I took for dinner that night at the Nelsons'. It was a nice little party, with Helen and Lawrence and Rob Austin. Dr Nelson went to bed after a while and let his household carry on. Helen and I gave Lawrence a few dancing lessons because they are both going to a dance next week and he got on quite nicely. Then we listened to the end of the wireless service and sang *God Save the King* and drank hot punch. Everyone had brought something to put into it. Teddy and I brought half a wine glass of brandy and somebody else brought a lemon and the result oddly enough was not nearly so horrid as usual, principally because someone had plonked a bottle of orangeade in with the rest, which somewhat drowned the taste.

There is now a chance that Teddy may go to Durham. If we are offered it we will have to go because Teddy is so disheartened by being here all the time, but I do hope we won't. It will mean amongst other things another great barn of a house and constant servant problems because there are no servants. All the people in the Close at Durham are living in their kitchens and have shut up all the other rooms. Teddy would hate it. And I very much doubt if he would like the people any more than those in Newcastle, being a southerner.

I hear talk of the invasion being well away by the middle of the month. Apparently the cold does not matter much, what is important is to have a reasonable period of darkness. If so it will have to commence soon, because it very suddenly gets much lighter in February. I am wondering myself if they are waiting for the Russians to take Poland. Anyway by the time they have all finished there will be very few people left to fight for, as the technique is to flatten out everything by air first and then send in troops under cover of the air attack. Then again Sir Percy suggests the Russians may finish off the Germans for us and we may not have to invade.

I wonder if you are still in Wales, or if you have been moved and what they will do with you. I will write again soon. Helen sends her love.

With love from Aunt Molly

JANUARY 5, CHISWICK

My dearest Otto,

I am very glad you have gone to Gloucestershire. It is one of the nicest counties (except Hertfordshire or Somerset) and you will find the country people more backward than the Welsh but quite nice.

The children are all here and some of us have had a 24-hour flu. I am writing now while recovering because next week I shall be very busy again. This letter is being written under difficulties as Helen is telling Hans's fortune again and it is being done across the typewriter, if you know what I mean.

Some people think the invasion will come from Persia and that the talk of all the American generals over here is a blind. On the other hand, invasion barges are all coming up the river and taking down armoured cars. I think there will be a lot of invasions all at the same moment in different places.

We are quickly eating our way through the rabbits now and Anthea is cleverly making fur gloves out of the skins.

Teddy preached at St Paul's Cathedral today and some of the children went to hear him. Irene had a Guides' parade. All our Christmas decorations have come down and the house looks very light without the ivy. I do not consider they were a great success this year. I am looking forward to hearing about your new company.

With love from Aunt Molly

P.S. Just got a letter from you – will answer soon.

*Helen telling Hans's fortune across Molly's typewriter.*

My dearest Otto,

We are coming to the end of the holidays. I am altering clothes and trying to make people pack trunks. Helen and Lawrence went to the dance at Hertford. Helen loved it as there were two Highland regiments to dance with, but as Lawrence cannot dance he had to clump with other boys in the same position in 'the bar', which sounds bad, but as they could only purchase cheese straws and lemonade they did not come to much harm.

They had a question on *The Brains Trust*[83] this week about writing letters. Someone asked if cheap books and the daily papers had not destroyed the art of letter writing. Joad said they had, because if someone had a good idea, instead of writing it to one friend he would write it for money to a paper or magazine. People agreed or disagreed with this, but no one gripped the fact that most people

---

83   *The Brains Trust* was a BBC radio programme with panellists Cyril Joad (a philosopher and psychologist), Julian Huxley (a biologist) and A B Campbell (a retired naval officer). Each weekly show generated over four thousand letters from listeners.

write letters not to diffuse good ideas but to keep in touch with people they cannot speak to. I think none of them can have children at school or sons in the military.

It is very foggy here. Yesterday it was so thick that Miss Coverley lost her way coming home. As the buses had stopped, the underground was packed and she had to wait for three trains till she could get into one. Then at Hammersmith it was so thick that directly one lost the sight of the kerb edge, everything was lost. Today, which is Sunday, is as bad as ever again.

I got Helen two new dresses the other day. She is a very satisfactory person to buy clothes for because she always looks so nice in them. The woman in the shop was full of sympathy for the coupon difficulties with children because she has three herself, mixed twins of 17 and a boy of 12. No handing down clothes there – they all need new ones each time.

I have just heard from one of the billeting officers in charge of evacuating civilians from the south coast before an invasion of the Continent. They have all been told to hold themselves in readiness as from tomorrow. They may let the schools get their travelling over first and then evacuate the towns, or we may not be allowed Easter holidays for schools. I wish it would start, I must say. It is a horrid thing to have hanging over one's head all the time.

Helen and Lawrence have gone to tea with the Austins. Mr A is rather difficult as he does not like having people in the house and will rush off to hide in the washhouse when he hears anyone at the door.

With love from Aunt Molly


JANUARY 14, CHISWICK

My dearest Otto,

I am sorry I have not had time to answer your letter before. The children have been returning to school and we've spent most of the week lugging suitcases down to the bus stop. I am now writing the letters that should have been written during the last month and sending off parcels of forgotten clothes.

Yesterday Lawrence and I took Helen to Waterloo Station. Sherborne boys' and girls' schools were all going and Helen's school and two prep schools, so there was a great long train full of children. A few very disconcerted American soldiers tried to get in but had to retire in disorder. I don't know what happened to them in the end. Most of the Sherborne boys had bicycles with them, which added to the congestion.

The day before that (Wednesday) I took Lawrence out because I had not been able to go anywhere with him this holiday. We had a lovely time going by train to Mansion House and walking to the Guildhall, though we could not go in because the Great Hall was bombed and the rest was being used for a meeting. We wandered in the direction of Barts [St Bartholomew's Hospital] and came to the gaunt skeleton of a church, St Giles Cripplegate, standing in the middle of about an acre of country that looked flat from a distance but turned out to be entirely composed of the foundations and cellars of bombed buildings that had been cleared away. Behind the church was a fire station and they had a small farm there with ducks and chickens. We went on again to another skeleton church standing up stiff and bare against the sky. Barts lies just outside the bombed area and even the lovely Tudor gateway of the church there [St Bartholomew the Great] has survived.

We could not go inside, so walked through the meat market. I think there is only a small portion used for meat now and the rest contains Army stores. After that we crossed another devastated area and came into the great diamond merchants' haunt, Hatton Garden. This is rather an exciting place with exotic-looking people walking about and rabbis talking Yiddish. In Leather Lane we found a small unofficial market. One man had a barrow of trinkets – rosaries, bags, spectacles, little boxes etc – and another was doing a brisk trade in watch parts. Yet another was selling anything you can think of to do with microscopes and one very talkative fellow was selling flints for firelighters. He was very funny and exceedingly clever. There were about 30 men, myself and one other woman listening to him. He begged us passionately not to be taken in by all the dud flints one could buy for a few pence, but to try his brand, which cost more but always lit. "Here is something to take home to mother" he cried, "which she will really appreciate and use!" After that we turned right, got lost and came out into civilisation via Staple Inn. We walked towards the river and stopped to listen to a man begging his "fellow workers" not to be content with their lot. He was not so fluent as the man with the flints, but made up for his lack of words with the most wonderful hand play and gesticulations. We landed up in the end by Bush House and went home from there.

I am sorry you have been on fatigue for so long. It must be beastly. Perhaps you will be able to get your section together and make them friendly. I wish you were still doing lumbering, because although it is dull and hard work it means you are out in the open.

Teddy says the invasion will not happen till April but does not say what makes him think that. Personally I think it will not take place until the coast towns have been evacuated.

With love from Aunt Molly

**After a long lull, the Germans resume raids on London on January 21.**

FEBRUARY 5, CHISWICK

My dearest Otto,

I am awfully sorry and really did not mean to sound gloomy when you telephoned. It was so very nice, because your letter arrived exactly on the 2$^{nd}$ [Molly's birthday] and then it was lovely hearing first from Patience, then you. Your voice was so clear you might have been in the next room. Patience sounded as if she was speaking through a swab of cotton wool.

Uncle Edward goes away for his 10 days' holiday tomorrow after church. He has been feeling rotten lately and I hope he will be better when he gets back. Miss Coverley is looking for a flat. Ilse and Irene are finding themselves rooms, so I shall shut up the top passage, especially as there have been a few raids. If they continue, we will get more East End evacuees. Fortunately I am well up in delousing children's heads and dealing with people who are not used to indoor sanitation. Up till now I have been very lucky with my inmates, but there is no reason why this should last. No, that is not gloomy, only common sense.

The Friday before last we had a fairly noisy time, but it was mostly our guns. Chiswick had four unexploded bombs, one with no fuse, so they had evidently been made by foreign labour in Germany. Last Thursday we had a very fine raid. I was fire-watching so saw it all, commencing at 5 am with half an hour at the docks, where they dropped a lot of stuff and several fires started. Then all the searchlights began to point in this direction. Silver fingers in bunches all round the sky bent towards Chiswick, first those in the distance, then those nearer and nearer. A couple of planes crossed by this house but they did not trouble about us, they were busy raiding somewhere far away right across the river. I had a good view of flares, phosphorus and fires. It was all over by 6.10. I had not been out in a raid for 18 months and it was interesting seeing how things had changed. The phosphorus was new to me, also the type of flare now used.

Everyone here is being asked to knit vests for babies in occupied countries. They must all be done by the end of March. One theory is that each soldier is to be given a vest to hand on to a baby in France or Holland, or wherever he happens to land during the invasion.

With love from Aunt Molly

*Vests for babies abroad."*

**The air attacks in February are the worst since May 1941. Molly dashes off the following note with a blunt pencil on a torn strip of paper.**

FEBRUARY 15, CHISWICK

My dearest Otto,

Just to say we are still all right. I am in the underground now going to Liverpool Street to find times of trains to send Anthea to the country tomorrow. Patience is not coming home – it is not fit here for children. Bombs have caught the railway somewhere after Ealing, so I do not think you will be able to come down today or Thursday. It was lovely seeing you last week so one must not grumble.

Patience will be so disappointed not coming home for her birthday, poor little girl.

I want to send this now as it was rather extra noisy last night. I am so afraid they will try again for the Lep [a works on Church Wharf] before I get Anthea away. Having a child in the house makes these raids absolutely nerve-wracking.

For goodness sake look after yourself.

With love from Aunt Molly.

**Otto is now in Iver, Buckinghamshire, less than 15 miles from Chiswick. Molly is out when he arrives unexpectedly at the Vicarage.**

FEBRUARY 18, CHISWICK

My dearest Otto,

I was so frightfully disappointed at missing you. I had only taken Anthea to the station. You cannot ring me up. Our line was cut during the first big raid and they are not mending them again yet. Can you come next Tuesday? If you are coming any other day will you send a wire and if possible give the time.

Every day makes travelling more difficult – I took two hours getting back from Liverpool Street today. Uncle Edward also had trouble returning from his holiday. If the raids get any hotter, we will not be here at all.

With love from Aunt Molly

**Otto and Molly have met in London, probably near Paddington Station.**

MARCH 4, CHISWICK

My dearest Otto,

It was lovely seeing you last weekend. I hope you got back all right. It took me over 1½ hours to get home because I tried to avoid a break in the line at Ladbroke Grove Station and went all over the place by mistake. I felt much better seeing you.

I went to do a little nursing at the Hays, who have been bombed. They were both cut by glass and bandaged, Heather with her arm in a sling and a great plaster all over her forehead. Wherever she goes she hears people wondering how it happened. After that I saw a family who had been bombed out twice in two days. They took some of the children's clothes I had in store. I tried to get them to take your Australian suit, but even a twice bombed-out boy would not look at it.

On Friday Uncle Edward and I went to see the little girls. They are all right and Anthea has settled down well at the new school and finds herself quite high in the class[84]. It was frightfully cold in the country and everything was rather difficult. We then went to see Amwell Bury, which we had been told was 'heavily bombed', but found only a few broken windows.

People seem to think the invasion will not start this month, so perhaps you will get your leave. I have been lucky to see you often.

---

84 Because of the bombing, Anthea left Colet school in Hammersmith to join Patience at The Barn School in Much Hadham, Hertfordshire.

So many women have sons who get little leave even if they are still in England.

I've heard something rather funny about two of my cousins. One was in India at the outbreak of war and joined up from there, the other went out two years ago. The oldest boy was going with his men from Africa to Asia Minor. They camped for the night at one of the usual sites, where they met some gunners journeying in the opposite direction. One of them was the other brother. They had not met for six years and the younger boy was so surprised he literally could not speak for five minutes. Later on they met again and had a leave together and wrote a joint letter home.

I have had trouble with the livestock on this estate. One of the hens had to be dosed and my lovely new doe got out and of course found the little deformed rabbit that runs loose about the garden and is called Billy Boy. The result of this will be awful deformed baby rabbits. Our telephone is on again, I am glad to say.

This seems a very disjointed and unsatisfactory letter. I will write again soon. There have been so many interruptions I lost the thread of what I was going to say. I wish you could have leave on your birthday. I am sorry you are still so unhappy.

With love from Aunt Molly

*Mothers' Union members admiring a fresh lemon to be raffled for the Red Cross.*

My dearest Otto,

All leave seems to be stopped. It is disappointing that you cannot come home, but the same applies to everyone so one cannot grumble. I am sorry you are stuck painting camouflage and hope your eyes are not too bad.

Philip Rae-Scott is home, discharged from the Army. He went to India as a Tommy under troopship conditions and it finished him off. I hope when the war is over that some of these more educated men who went out as privates will be able to get conditions changed. English troopships have always been a disgrace. I suppose it would be the same for other nations, but we are the only country that must send troops for long sea voyages and we should have learned to organise better by this time. Also in the English Army the difference between officers and men is quite old-fashioned. The Canadian Army and our Air Force do not make such distinction between officers and men and our Army should come into line.

We are still having trouble in the farmyard. The sitting hen has broken two eggs and now only has four and the un-sitting hen refuses to eat and is looking very pale. She has not laid an egg for some time, moping because her companion is sitting and will not play with her.

Everyone is home for the holidays and I am again immersed in children's clothes. Everyone is trying to wear each other's because we are short of coupons. There are certain things, such as my dark blue coat, which can be worn by everyone. Patience is taking it back to school and Helen is having your little white Austrian coat instead.

The Heatons have found a cottage in Surrey and we will share the rent so the children can go down in case of raids. Neville is there now with his little boys while Cecily is in London for a few days getting The Hollies in order. He will live in The Hollies and she and the children will evacuate to Cheltenham.

I am sorry – the paper has caught under the end of this machine. The children have all been using it and it is rather wonky now.

Hans has gone for an all-day walk. Last time he went to Uxbridge [12 miles from Chiswick]. Lawrence is trying to find out about camps for the summer holidays.

As I write there are two huge, dark and shapeless landing barges slowly gliding down the river, looking very sinister.

I wonder what is going to happen and when. Anyway I wish it would come soon.

With love from Aunt Molly

**Otto is now in Sennybridge, Wales, with Canadian Pioneers.**

MARCH 17, CHISWICK

My dearest Otto,

I am sorry this paper is so grubby, but it is pre-war and must be used up.

Herbert writes that Aliens can now change their names. I hope he will be content to translate his and will not insist on finding some weird and wonderful new name. We have all discussed it and think you should change yours. The authorities recommend it and after all it is only a nom-de-plume in case they send you abroad. You could join Myra in the ranks of the Walkers, I expect. Even if you were sent to an army of occupation after the fighting was over, it would be better not to have a German name.

The weather is so lovely here. I wish we could exchange some of your suffering for our sun. The seeds need watering so badly and it hardly seems worthwhile planting anything.

Sennybridge does not sound a very suitable place to send Canadians. They are wild enough when there is something for them to do. If you can get talking to any of them do ask all about Canada. I do so much want to know what your officers and non-commissioned officers are like, also what you do for training. If you have to march for miles it will be a lovely country to do it in.

We had a woman to breakfast today whose daughter and her six children are all returning from Canada, where they went at the beginning of the war. She said they have had the worst winter in Canada for 200 years, with blizzards and awful winds ripping doors and windows off houses. The family were in more danger with the weather there than they would have been from bombs here.

No, I am not worried about your going out of England. I shall miss not having you back on leave, but everyone is in the same position when it comes to that. I am so absolutely sure you're supposed to help in the world after the war that I do not think you will be killed.

Helen, Irene and Patience went to a fire-fighting practice last night. They were representing the Rev Rich, Mrs Rich and Mr Elmslie, who were all too busy or too ill to go.

I had a Mothers' Union meeting here in the afternoon. Someone brought a lemon and raffled it for the Red Cross. We had none of us seen a lemon for ages and passed it round. It smelled so lovely. Last night I used up the last little tin of concentrated lemon essence. It was sent from America a long time ago [Sept 1941] and made from real lemon and so needed a lot of sugar. I'll write again soon.

With love from Aunt Molly


MARCH 20, CHISWICK

My dearest Otto,

I think the invasion will begin in the middle of May or in June. I think they will try to get everyone placed before then and you may not even come back to say goodbye. If you get a chance of even a few hours, do take it. I should not mind your going out so much if they had not already sent you to Australia.

Did you receive my birthday letter? I will try to get you something nice for your birthday, because it will be the last thing I can give you for years.

Helen is going to a conference at Hammersmith on reconstruction after the war. I am so glad. It lasts several days and is for people between 15 and 20. After the last war we were all unwanted and more or less told there was nothing for us to do. This time it looks as if young people are to be allowed a chance to help. If older people had been able or willing to use us after the last war, we might not have had this war.

Both black rabbits have had their babies. The mothers pull out their fur to mix with the hay bedding and make the most lovely soft snuggly nests for their little ones. When you look in the nesting box you can see nothing but a heap of softness. Every now and again it heaves in a most exciting way and you know a baby rabbit is moving about.

Mrs Austin is going to help in a canteen for American soldiers. If she likes going, then after the Easter holiday I will go too. I feel as you may go abroad I should like to help other soldiers who are away from their homes. I hope some woman would help you if you were in that sort of position.

If you want things like socks, send me an Airgraph. I can get them from the Chiswick Depot. We have done such a lot of knitting for them and they like to get things sent out to people from Chiswick, if possible. One woman heard from her son in Central Africa that he had not had socks for months and they sent some off at once.

With love from Aunt Molly


MARCH 23, CHISWICK

My dearest Otto,

Helen thinks she will have to leave school next term because she will not get her remove. Teddy is again thinking of the Newcastle business. He is going up to look at houses. We would not move till after the summer holidays.

Ilse's cousin Brendt is one of those people who seem more or less permanently on leave because his wife is having a baby. I wish you would marry and have some children, then you might get extra leave, too. I should so love a little curly-haired grandchild with piano legs.

Let me know if you are thinking about a new name. Only, please, I cannot call you 'Tom'. You said you had preconceived ideas of Ottos as fat people with big tummies and necks in rolls. My Toms are thin and dirty with broken teeth. Does Myra really object to 'David'? Perhaps till after the war you should just be a number. The nameless private. You could be in *Picture Post*: "The nameless private gets up in the morning, eats his breakfast, drills, makes a road, has his supper, goes to bed." You will have hundreds of letters from girls wanting to marry you and old ladies wanting to mother you.

I don't mind if you marry several girls, but if you take on another adoptive mother I shall be very cross. Yes, I know that is all silly and beside the point. I just wish so much you could come home and I am terrified of your being sent away and never coming back, but as one cannot do anything about it – well.

With love from Aunt Molly

MARCH 25, CHISWICK

My dearest Otto,

This will be a short letter because I am knitting socks and stockings against time and should really be doing them now.

Helen is back from her conference and the house is very full again. I have pushed off five of the family on bicycles. This had to be done very quickly because Gem said she was coming down for the afternoon and I knew she would want to go too. She will take on an elder-sister attitude to my children and order them about, which causes trouble. Gem has sat for her nursing exam and thinks she has passed. Teddy says they will not plough any girl now and I'm sure he is right as they want nurses too badly. Even Miss Coverley and I have to register – she because she has always done nursing off and on and I because, in the dim ages during the last war, I rushed round a convalescent hospital.

This letter has been temporarily held up by the arrival of Anthea with the two Austin girls. They all dashed to the piano and made Bonzo play chopsticks and have now left as swiftly as they came. I sent them to see our baby rabbits. I wish you could see them too.

I haven't done much lately except cook large meals and meet trains, so there is nothing to tell you. In fact I wrote a bit of your weekly letter yesterday and it was so dull I started another.

Here are the cyclists back again for tea.

With love from Aunt Molly

My dearest Otto,

Thank you so much for the chocolate, which has been put away till Easter Sunday. I think there is a lot there, more than a month's ration, which is lovely.

It is raining hard now, which means all the seeds will now come up and we will be able to re-plant. The last week has been quite wonderful, very hot. Everyone shed their woolly vests and now most of them have been in bed with sick attacks.

We all went to Kew the other day and met the Heatons for lunch. It was lovely and warm and the blossom trees were wonderful. Crowds of people came in at about three o'clock when we were coming out. I think Kew will be very crowded this year as so few places are open and cinema seats have gone up in price.

I am wondering if you will get leave and if you are still concreting or if you have started training again.

There seems so little to say this week. I have done nothing but re-foot stockings and socks. Lawrence needs so many clothes now that he is at Marlborough. Fortunately they have a school shop in the town and the boys can get the school uniform there without coupons. I don't see how anyone would get a suit of clothes otherwise.

We have had several warnings lately, but nothing has happened so far.

Helen has gone to a rehearsal of an Easter play. She is to be an angel. Lawrence calls it "dress rehearsal for the afterlife". We will all go and see her next week. Mrs Speitzer [a refugee who cleaned at the Vicarage] has blossomed out into a well-trained soprano, so I think we will go and hear her too, in the near future. She was given an introduction to the choir of the Chiswick Poly. I am glad because she will meet other people who are fond of music.

Did I tell you Bonzo attacked a Chow dog and was bitten in the foot and we had to take him to the vet? They told Patience that he would have to be poulticed every hour and brought back again at the end of five days to have the whole toenail removed. Well, Patience did her best, but it is almost impossible to poultice a dog and as soon as you put on a bandage the animal licks it off. I think the foot is getting better of its own account and so will not need an operation.

This afternoon I'm taking the family and Cecily Heaton to the other side of the river. The last time I went there it was with you and Lawrence, during your first leave more than a year ago.

I am sorry this letter is so deadly. Also it seems quite horribly untidy.

With love from Aunt Molly

**Otto is now in Saffron Walden, Essex and is able to visit the Vicarage regularly on brief leaves.**

APRIL 1, CHISWICK

My dearest Otto,

I was glad to get your letter and new address. Yes, Saffron Walden really is in the depth of the country. I should think you are more cut away than in Wales and the locals are even simpler than the Welsh as they have no national culture to keep up. I always think there is something rather fascinating about that countryside, although I do not like it because there are not enough trees.

Here in Chiswick things are getting green and fresh. The chestnut hanging over the wall has pale green leaves unfolding like small hands stretching their fingers towards the sun.

The little girls have gone to Haslemere to stay with the Heatons. Teddy took them down and said they were quite contented. Helen returned to Chiswick on Friday. I was lucky, because there were two trains arriving in the morning from Sherborne, one at 11.09 and the other at 11.45. The people waiting for the first one had to stand in the cold for almost ¾ of an hour and in the end the two trains arrived together at 11.50. Helen and I walked over Hungerford footbridge to Westminster. We had a simply lovely view of the city. From there we walked to Trafalgar Square, where they were still holding the Salute the Soldier Week[85]. We listened to the band and

---

85    Greater London's Salute the Soldier Week ran from March 25 to April 1 with a challenge to raise £165 million for the war effort.

later on heard that Michael Redgrave had spoken to the crowds and a famous Negro had sung spirituals. Then we had lunch at the 'Help Yourself' [a canteen of the WVS] and went to see the Hays, who have left their bombed house and are now residing in a flat while they look for another house. I hope they will find somewhere suitable soon, perhaps in Chiswick.

We had one scare of a raid last week but nothing happened and Mr Owen and I discussed new housing schemes for a very cold hour in the Mall till the all clear went just about 4 am.

With love from Aunt Molly

APRIL 8, CHISWICK

My dearest Otto,

We are all going to join the little girls and the Heatons at Hindhead, near Haslemere for a week on the 20th, so do not come as the house will be shut up. I will write and give you our address. If the second front breaks out while we are there we could be stuck for 10 days. Not that it will matter much, there will be nothing to do in London. I do not even think we will have the doubtful pleasure of being bombed.

Miss Coverley has left for her new flat in Barrowgate Road. It is very nice and I think she will like being on her own. She has some good furniture that was kept in the borough storage place during the time she was here, lovely old chairs and family glass and a lacquer cabinet that she is going to sell. She should get a lot for it. Helen, Lawrence and I went and fitted her into her rooms. We had quite a busy time heaving furniture about and laying carpets. It is queer and dull with her rooms at the Vicarage empty, although Anthea has gone back into her old bedroom. In a way it is a good thing, as I do need another room in the holidays.

It is awfully cold here. Our brown hen is sitting and Mrs Townsend has given us six eggs. The hen will not come into a hen coop but insists on sitting on the coke pile, so we have had to build a coop round her and over the coke too.

Irene is to stay with Miss Coverley for the last three days of her time in London. She has left the Guides and is now on a three-week training course at the BBC, which will then send her up north. They are told all about the company as well as shown how the typing must done.

With love from Aunt Molly

My dearest Otto,

Thank you very much for sending the wonderful wood for the coop. It all arrived just as we returned from Haslemere and just as three of the chicks have hatched out. The fourth egg I think will be a dud. We also bought four day-old chicks to give the hen to look after with her others. The babies are so sweet and until accepted by the hen, have to be kept on a hot-water bottle at night. There are two dark and two fair ones.

Haslemere is a lovely place, all fir trees, silver birches and gorse bushes. The ground is sandy and golden-looking and the colouring is warm and sunny, though the place is so high it is really cold. We had two perfect days and sat and got very burnt and caught colds in the sun.

Cecily's mother, Mrs Alabaster, is also staying. She is a pond-life expert and takes Anthea to the Devil's Punchbowl where they fish up and examine algae and spirostomum and other pond life under her microscope.

We also saw gliders there. I had never seen them before. One evening there was a fire in the woods nearby and the children went to help three fire brigades and a rabble of people put it out.

I wonder if you will get any leave next week. We are going out to supper on Tuesday and I will give Lawrence the telephone number in case you turn up. We are going to meet the late Bishop of London[86], who will not want to see me at all but will be quite contented talking to Teddy.

---

86  The 'late' Bishop of London was Geoffrey Fisher, who in 1944 was appointed Archbishop-Elect of Canterbury after the sudden death of William Temple. Years earlier, while in Fisher's Rolls-Royce with Teddy, Molly broke a jar of marmalade she had bought at a charity fair and it spread all over the car's carpeted floor. Edward claimed he was never made a bishop because of it.

There does not seem to be anything to say. I am very busy mending and altering and marking school clothes for the children and arranging for various things to happen.

Hoping to see you again before long.

With love from Aunt Molly

**The Allied invasion of France begins on D-Day, June 6. Soon after the Germans retaliate with V1 flying bombs targeted at England. In Chiswick, the Cubitts Yacht Basin is hit on June 18 and 12 more V1s cause great damage until the end of August.**

JUNE 23, CHISWICK

My dearest Otto,

Don't worry about flying bombs. They are no worse than an ordinary landmine, the reason why people dislike them so much is that they think they are 'uncanny'. It is really like being shelled and in the last war the shelling of Paris got the Parisians down more than the raids. Anyway we have none in the Mall. They mostly come over our house and on into London or explode on the south side of the river. They are interesting to watch as a mechanical device. As destructive agents, they do not do nearly the harm the Germans had expected.

Now the anti-aircraft barrage has stopped at night we can all sleep in peace, which is the principal thing. Most people had got into the habit of sleeping through the bangs and some – Mr Elmslie, for instance, who no longer hears the alarm clock through his slumbers – sleep more than they ever did before. He cannot even wake for services now and I am sure he never came out for his fire-watch last night at 3 am when I went in.

We had Blois Johnson[87] to supper on Monday, also Teddy's friend Mrs Findlay. We gave them a first-class view of 'doodlebugs' as an

---

87  Francis Nelson Blois Johnson RNR had served aboard the HMS *Clyde* and was mentioned in despatches. In 1944 he was in London at the Admiralty while recovering from a wound. He was possibly a little bit in love with Molly.

entertainment and they all enjoyed it very much. Blois had never seen them before because during a raid he is always so busy dishing out tea to the ladies in the block of flats where he lives. They all come to him when they get frightened. He is pleased when they say, "Oh Commander Johnson, now you are back we feel quite safe again!"

I will write again soon. I am glad you're not still camouflaging tents, but I shall miss your coming to London every week. Are my letters censored?

With love from Aunt Molly

JUNE 27, CHISWICK

My dearest Otto,

We are all right here, only everyone is slightly jumpy about the doodles. If you think of it as being shelled it is all right. If you will persist in thinking you are a private target for the Devil, as lots of people do, you get very edgy. The thing seen from the ground, if you are standing underneath, looks like a cross with a fire in its tail, so people imagine it is a sort of black magic like they used to practice in the Middle Ages, when they turned a crucifix upside down and got a renegade priest to say the Mass backwards.

Actually you need not worry, because these things are not nearly so bad as the raids we had in February. I did hate those. If the doodle comes near it sounds like an express train over your head, but the engine always stops about a minute before it explodes, so there is heaps of time to stand behind a wall and out of the blast. They do less damage than a landmine and the crater is not so large as that of a bomb.

I had a scene with Hans because he would insist on sleeping on the top storey during one of the nights when they were obviously trained in this direction. We had arranged for him to sleep downstairs after two had come fairly near and then at about 4 am one fell not far from the baths and in the later morning I discovered His Lordship sleeping where I had told him definitely not to sleep, i.e. in his own bed. So I told him firmly and coldly that he would in future have to live elsewhere, as he was too large for me to carry downstairs and he would not go of his own accord and I could not be responsible if he would not do as he was told. Next night all was quiet and one could have slept happily and safely on the roof, but Hans and bedclothes came downstairs. He now sleeps on the ground floor and says he is quite comfortable.

Hans is still revising and Helen is doing her exams. I am glad that Anthea has left London. St Paul's are doing their exams in the shelters and the other day just as they had finished, a bomb dropped a little way away and all their papers were blown out the door. They were all right and were collected again.

With love from Aunt Molly

JULY 1, CHISWICK

My dearest Otto,

It would be nice to hear your silly voice again. I am usually in every evening before the news as I have Neville Heaton here now Cecily and the boys have evacuated to Cheltenham. He comes for supper. After the news I sometimes take Bonny out.

I saw *The Bridge of San Luis Rey* with Irene and Miss Coverley. The newsreel was about the calling-up of America's 45 year olds, my contemporaries, who slapped each other on the back and playfully pushed each other out of trains and dug each other continually in the ribs and generally behaved like 12 year olds. Very refreshing, but a bit odd to a European.

With love from Aunt Molly

JULY 6, CHISWICK

My dearest Otto,

Don't ring up till Saturday or Sunday. Chiswick Lane caught a doodle and the rest shelters are all open and I am frightfully busy and will be not be in evenings for a bit.

All well here.

Love, Aunt Molly

My dearest Otto,

The typewriter is out of order so I must do my best to be legible by hand.

I went away Wednesday to see the children and came home Thursday to find half of Chiswick Lane taken down by a doodlebug. Our end is untouched. The thing had glided in over Hammersmith. No one of course heard anything till the bang came. Two people were killed and there are many homeless. We had 50 in the rest centre and had to open the shelters in Boston House. These shelters were beautifully fitted up with bunks, pillows, mattresses and blankets, all wringing wet. We had to get the damp ones out and put in aired stuff. It took a long time and was rather hard work.

One of the 'bombed-outs' had relations at Epsom wanting to take her in, but she would not budge because she had lost her parrot. The bird was eventually found and she went on her way. Her home and everything she had was gone, but her great worry was the parrot. It reminded me of your story of the man who, after losing everything, nearly lost his life fighting for his coat that had been stolen.

It rained hard the day after the bombing, but people had to stay in their roofless houses otherwise their stuff would be looted. I think looters should be shot, as they were at the beginning of the war in Russia. All the people housed in the first five days in the rest centre have been found homes and now the place is shut.

If our house gets doodled, could you obtain compassionate leave?

Things here are all slightly difficult. Bonzo's back is covered with raw places and I shall have to take him to the vet tomorrow. Dinah is having kittens any moment. Your bedroom is full of Neville Heaton's cockerels. Helen writes to say she thinks she has passed her School Certificate. She is very pleased with herself and I am told this is a very dangerous attitude to adopt and usually means one has failed.

Doodles must be in short supply as we have not had many in the last couple of days. Nonetheless I saw hundreds of women and children evacuating when I went through Victoria. Cecily says there are so many new arrivals at Cheltenham that food is short.

The minor excitement here is the court case of the Adamses and Morleys, who lived in the Vicarage for nine months during the Blitz. Their present landlord wants them out of his flat. When at the Vicarage they were quiet, respectable people, but lately they all seem to have become devils and behave so badly to their landlord it is upsetting his health. It is all very queer and I cannot understand the change. Anyway he is trying to get them out and has brought the case to court. I have not heard the result.

With love from Aunt Molly

My dearest Otto,

This is your birthday present, with my love. It is so late because they don't make 'twiddly pencils' [propelling pencils] any more now, so one can only pick them up second-hand. I am sorry it is not of a more sober hue, but that cannot be helped, either. A pretend gold one was all I could get.

Thank you for ringing up. You sounded so clear I could not think you were speaking from Essex. Since the excitement of the bomb in Chiswick Lane nothing has happened. Irene and I are lunching in town tomorrow and going to see *The Forgotten Village*. Even the films have become quite stagnant, either very bad or very old. Actually I think no one ever goes to the picture houses or the theatre now. The other day Hans got into *The Lisbon Story* for 3/- without even waiting at the door.

Last week a flying bomb caught an oil factory on the riverside and now there are casks of oil floating about and the water is covered in oil. The poor swans are sitting on the island all brown and filthy. Oil on their plumage will kill them in a short time, but very often someone sends the swans to Richmond to give them a bath. I hope they will either do this or come and kill them, because being oily must be such a horrid way to die.

Three kittens arrived yesterday and we are keeping two this time. One is black with a short tail like mother, the other tabby with a shortish tail, presumably like father.

Neville says thousands of teachers and doctors will be wanted after the war and why don't you take a government training and become one or the other? He is always trying to make people into teachers because working on education reform, he visualises the armies of teachers that he needs but knows will never turn up. It is odd how Neville, who has to meet and talk to so many people publicly, can remain so shy in private.

With love from Aunt Molly

JULY 22, CHISWICK

My dearest Otto,

Gem is interviewing at a hospital in Oxford with the idea of going there in the autumn. Herbert has written from Italy about melons, a fruit he seems just to have discovered. Hans has taken his exam and goes about white and silent. I am glad he goes to camp soon. He bought three new ties last week. One pretty blue one he does not like, one grey one and one grey and red.

You will be glad to hear that one of my rabbits has had more little ones and that Bonny, whose sore back is better, is supposed to have caught another rat. We don't believe this last rumour and can only conclude that he found a dead one lying about and told Miss Coverley that he had killed it.

There is no more news. Tomorrow I am collecting Patience from Much Hadham for the day. I hope you are quite well again.

With love from Aunt Molly

JULY 24, CHISWICK

My dearest Otto,

I took Patience as far as St Margarets on her way back to school on Sunday evening after tea, putting her into her train at the little station there. The train was just bursting with Land Girls all returning to their hostels after having had 36 hours in their homes in the East End. They were all remarkably alike, with fair bleached hair done high on top and bright lips and nails. They seemed to be enjoying themselves. The posher girls generally live on a farm or in a billet and work by themselves and the others choose to live in a hostel and work in a gang. I must say they all looked 'very healthy', as you would say. When I had seen Patience off I went to have supper with my sister-in-law Mary at Rookery House (mixed salad and strawberries and cream – wonderful). Next day I went with her to look at some of the estate cottages, which are busy tumbling down. We will have to do a lot to them to put them right. That is the worst of cottages. They certainly look lovely from the outside and the gardens are bright and full of flowers, but there is always something wrong.

We are having perfectly lovely weather. I do hope it is better for you, too. The rabbits are all well and I hope to have another family in a month's time. I think this bit of news will hearten you a lot.

With love from Aunt Molly

JULY 30, CHISWICK

My dearest Otto,

First I want to say I am sorry I said goodbye in that miserable way after you left. I did not mean to. I hope you got back all right and that the journey was not too long. I have heard awful stories about people's journeys. One of Helen's school friends left Somerset at 11 am one day and arrived at Norwich 2 am the next. On Friday Patience went to stay with my Aunt Mary near Ware. She was supposed to arrive in time for lunch and you can imagine our horror when they rang up at 2 to say she had not turned up. I was terrified and could not think what could have happened as we saw her into her train and the only change was at St Margarets, where she knows the whole village intimately. Well, we rang up stationmasters all along the line from Liverpool Street and were just about to ring the police when a call came through to say Patience had just walked in. They had a new porter on at Broxbourne, which is the junction and he made everyone get out of the Ware train and put them into the Bishop's Stortford train. Patience was sure he was wrong, but he would not let anyone remain in the train and bustled them all off to Essex. Fortunately Patience knows all the country round and got out at Burnt Mill, which was the first station and took a bus to Much Hadham.

Anthea looks much better than she has done for some time, but they say she must have her tonsils out. She is very thin and when we have Neville and Hans and Anthea all sitting at supper, Teddy and Helen and I feel almost awkwardly fat by contrast.

I think I hear a bomb coming up in the distance. They had one behind the Hammersmith Town Hall on the towing path by the river. It made a great mess and even The Doves[88] has been a bit shattered. They say there will be no beer next year because the flying bombs are all being brought down over the hop fields of Kent and naturally no hop-pickers will go out there. The hop-pickers are usually East Enders and the poor things know too much about flying bombs to want to have a holiday in their midst.

There is no news. Lawrence returns on Tuesday. Marlborough always does what the other schools do not do in the way of breaking up. I suppose it is such a big school they have special trains for the children anyway. They also have the City of London Boys' School, which was evacuated to the town and there must be over 1000 people to convey from Marlborough at the end of each term.

There is definitely nothing more to say.

With love from Aunt Molly

AUGUST 4, CHISWICK

My dearest Otto,

We have had rather a horrid time lately. Hans came back from camp with a poisoned hand. This of course meant poultices every two hours and endless successions of meals on a tray and very little time for anything else. Yesterday I had finished Hans's hand, rushed down to the town for more lint and returned to find Lawrence and Anthea looking rather white and scared. They said they had

---

88   The Doves, now The Dove, still exists as a riverside pub in Hammersmith. There has been a public house on the site since the 17th century.

found a dead baby in the grounds of Chiswick House. I went back with them and sure enough the poor little thing was very horribly dead and we told the police. Of course it was an awful shock for the children, especially for Anthea and I am afraid it may dent her subconscious or something. She is getting over it a bit now, but she was frightfully scared at first and the baby looked so horrid and a person of Anthea's age cannot easily understand about the biological reasons of decomposition and in the end I was horrified to find I had given her the idea that all the trees were made up of dead people. Actually of course in a roundabout way they are all made up of dead something or other, but children take things so literally. Lawrence had a bad fright as well but is all right again now.

With love from Aunt Molly

AUGUST 6, CHISWICK

My dearest Otto,

It will be awfully nice if you get some more leave. I am wondering if you will go to France. After all, there are so many people waiting over here to go.

Anne Croasdell heard from her husband in France last week. He said there was no news (the usual complaint) and that all the soldiers in the BLA [British Liberating Army] are insisting that they are in the Bloody Lunatic Asylum.

We had another bomb in the parish the night before last, with a lot of damage done to very many exceedingly nice houses, but only one slight casualty from glass. We know several people in the road so went to look them up. One of them had rescued a bombed-out puppy. It is a mongrel fox terrier, a bitch, unfortunately and they brought it back here. Meanwhile two stray black kittens have been 'planted' on us, so the three animals came at the same time. I cannot keep any of them as it is not possible to feed so many creatures. I already have a garden full of starving chicks and I kept two of Dinah's kittens this time.

Irene is here for a few days' holiday. In ten days Hans will find out about his exam and then goes for good. I shall miss him very much, but he and Teddy never got on. I shall have no one in the house for the autumn, so we will shut up most of the rooms and live in the study and dining room. Anyway it will save coal.

I shall try for a part-time job if the war is still on after the holidays, though work is not so easy to obtain now. Some of the munitions factories have actually closed and others are in peacetime work, so no new 'hands' are needed. As we have no troops here canteens are not wanted and the civilian canteens are already fully staffed.

Patience left for camp and has just written. Her letter has a real camp address, all numbers and letters, like the addresses you have. She is having a wonderful time. Lawrence goes tomorrow to stay at a friend's farm. All the children's luggage is missing, as usual. The difficulty is that Chiswick is not on any railway or railway van route. Everything has to go to Acton first and gets lost there.

With love from Aunt Molly

**Otto has joined the British Army and is now in France.**

AUGUST 9, CHISWICK

My dearest Otto,

Your letter arrived yesterday and I was so surprised. I had worked myself into a nice peaceful position thinking the Russians would do it all and you would not have to go abroad after all.

The two bombed-out cats have suddenly disappeared. I was very thankful, because five cats in a house are too much of a good thing. One saw CAT wherever one looked and there was a cat crying for food in every room. The bombed-out puppy, which is entirely untrained, is going to Mrs Stevens when we are sure the owners will not turn up. It is not possible for me to keep a lady fox terrier and Bonny together without letting them have puppies and the mixture would be a nightmare. I am going to buy a rough-haired Dax bitch and breed pups. I think I should make a little money that way. Bonny is getting very old and has mange and will have to go soon, but he is so sweet I should like to have some of his puppies before he dies.

Patience arrived back from camp yesterday with a badge as the best first-year camper. We are very proud of her. It appears she was the only person who could 'lash' and if you can't do that in a guide camp, you cannot get a tent up properly. As they all lived in tents, she must have been rather an important person.

I should so like to know what you are doing and where you are and what the place is like, but I know that is impossible. Quite apart from the censor, I think you will not be able to write much. I am ringing up Myra next time I get a letter and she will do the same for me – so if one of our letters goes astray we shall still know you are all right. God bless you.

With love from Aunt Molly

My dearest Otto,

I think it will be very noisy and hot and uncomfortable in France and there will be a great deal of hard work. Having you there has made us start taking an active interest in the news. We have bought an 'invasion map' and we look up the names of the places each day. Today on the films we saw a picture of a rest camp in Normandy that looked rather fun (bathing and riding etc), but I am afraid it will be a long time before you qualify for that, because all the people we saw resting had been out since D-Day.

We went to see *This Happy Breed*. I always disliked the name of the film because it sounds more like breeding dogs than the story of a human family. However Uncle Edward says it is a quotation from *Richard II*. Helen took Mrs Hay for her birthday present and then decided it would be good for her parents to see it, to help keep us young. It is quite typical Noël Coward, though not so good as *In Which We Serve*.

We have had a very quiet time here lately with almost no doodles. Our bombed-out puppy has gone permanently to Mrs Stevens and Neville has taken away his hens and the 14 young cockerels that I once kept in your room, thank goodness. The animals get so tame there is no holding them in. We were having tea in the garden and a hen walked up and snatched the cake from an old lady's hand. They are so bold, we cannot have a downstairs window open in case they should walk in. The other day six of them got into the house and mauled the sausages that were on the kitchen table, but evidently thought the same about them as you and Uncle Edward because they left them and went to attack the butter. They were just finishing off the rations for five people for a week when I came

*Neville's hens grew so bold that one snatched the cake from an old lady's hand.*

in. I was furious and said they would have to be killed, but I can do nothing about it as I cannot kill them myself and know no one else who can. I am afraid we have them with us till they die of old age, which takes about 11 years.

There is no news except that I bought Anthea and Patience some clothes the other day. Goodban's in Hammersmith is having a sale of 'blasted goods', which sounds rather good. Everyone is away. The Edwardses have left Suffolk House and the neighbours are always

*Molly shooing the hens out of the kitchen window after they had discovered the butter ration.*

rounding up their rabbits, which are constantly escaping in the absence of their mistress. Also they have left a dog that makes a noise like a whole zoo all day long.

The other day when the charlady, Mrs Speitzer, arrived in the morning she found our dining-room window open. She rushed to the Elwells and made Walter go back with her and hunt in all the rooms, because she thought a burglar was hiding about the house. In the end it turned out the French window in Uncle Edward's study had been blown open by the blast of a bomb about three miles away at the other side of the river.

The Heaton's garden has a lovely lot of mulberries. I pick them when I have time to spare but it takes ages and after gathering them one looks as if one had stepped straight out of a detective novel.

With love from Aunt Molly

My dearest Otto,

It was lovely getting your second letter. You say there is so little you are allowed to write, but with what we know from the papers I have gathered quite a lot. No, I am not worrying about you, because the Germans are retreating. If they stand still or advance I cannot promise to continue in this frame of mind. Yesterday we heard of the landing in the South of France. I hope you will get down there, the country is beautiful. I am sorry you did not get any letters from me, but I wrote each week and sent a paper in the middle of the week as usual. My butcher's wife, from whom I get all the news, says the war will not be over till the spring. I hope she is wrong.

Hans has failed his exam in one subject. He hopes to be able to take the whole thing over again in December and pass with honours, but will need an extension from the Poly. He took the exam at the worst time. On the day he sat for the Theory of Machines, the whole class had to dive under their desks when a doodle fell rather close.

Helen and all the other School Cert. people say they have failed their Certs. on the French. Apparently the French was all idioms and they none of them had been taught any. Anyway they do not get results till next month so everything is supposition.

Lawrence loved working on the farm and is going back in September.

They have washed all the oily swans and put them back clean and sparkling into the river. There is a fleet of about 20 cruising up and down by the island and they look better than they have for years. Our two new kittens are very sweet. Mrs Stevens is delighted with the bombed-out puppy. It is an enormous success and keeps her two boys, who are both now at home, happy for hours.

With love from Aunt Molly

AUGUST 18, CHISWICK

My dearest Otto,

What a good thing you rubbed up your French before going away. I wonder why they pay you in francs? The Americans in England are paid in dollars. I hope you will have time to wander about and see more of the country later on. What I remember of Normandy is miles of flat fields with scarlet poppies and brilliant blue chicory flowers growing among the corn and miles of white sand beaches stretching out to shallow green seas. There were a lot of lovely little crooked towns, most of them having had something vaguely to do with William the Conqueror. I am afraid most of these villages no longer exist.

I am sorry I addressed your last envelope to your old name. I think 'David' is lovely and do not even mind calling you that, if you like, but feel the change will be slightly difficult. I hope I may still call you Otto, at least for a while longer. I am glad you made the decision. As Teddy said, it is the fairest thing you can do for the next generation.

Everything goes on here as usual. Helen and I went to a lovely lunch-hour concert at the National Gallery and heard Gerald Moore accompany a tenor who sang about 24 of Schubert's songs. They have the concerts in a smallish room underground now because of the bombs. There were quite a number of people but nothing like what they used to have. A great many of the more expensive theatres have had to close down altogether and I wonder how the cinemas pay, they are completely empty in the afternoons as it is.

Helen is very disappointed because the friend she was going to stay with next week had to put her off owing to a flood of bombed-out relatives descending on them. Fortunately we have the swimming baths quite near and they have a good air-raid shelter, otherwise the holidays would be very dull for the children. It is lovely having them all home again and they are very good about the dullness of everything.

It is so very hot and we have to keep all the doors and windows tightly closed as the chickens continue to stampede all over the house, given the chance. Teddy has been digging the garden and tried to make me help, but so far I have refused. He has dug up the two allotments, plus the rhubarb and Lawrence's tomatoes. I was sorry to lose the rhubarb, but when Teddy gets going he is like a tank and there is no stopping him, he just digs through everything.

Peggy Owen has just had a nice little baby girl. Most of the people I know have girls, but they say a great many of the babies are boys. Both the Elwell girls have evacuated. The nursing home of St Mary's Convent is being evacuated too and that means getting 100 stretcher cases as well as nurses and sisters away. One of the slightly less ill inmates is probably coming here for a few days. I do not know where she will sleep – the cellar, the cloakroom, Helen's room and study are already full.

Someone was writing to the papers today saying he heard a nightingale singing all through the guns of Normandy. I wonder if you have heard any nightingales.

With love from Aunt Molly

AUGUST 25, CHISWICK

My dearest Otto,

Two letters from you arrived today. They seem to take about four days. We are very interested to hear you have seen a battle and wonder if there were tanks.

We are so glad Paris was mainly liberated by Parisians. We heard that piece of news in the cinema via a 'news flash' on the screen: "PARIS IS LIBERATED". We'd been to see a film called *A Canterbury Tale*, with many pictures of Kent and the cathedral and actors who were not film actors at all but ordinary people. It was all so fresh and really a lovely picture.

We saw a newsreel of French soldiers returning to France in their tanks and people running to throw flowers to them. I thought how lucky were the people who had a rejoicing country to return to.

It has been raining and thundering here. Lawrence has made a nightmare raft on which he and the little girls float up the Thames, to the envy of all the boys round. Yesterday they all came in like drowned rats and the house is still full of wet clothes and mud.

*Lawrence built a nightmare raft to float on the Thames.*

Chiswick has been surrounded by doodles. The Germans have got it into their heads that something of military importance lies here. Very few people have been hurt and the destruction is mostly to public property, but it is very tiring and restless having constant sirens wailing and roaring rockets overhead and thumps all round. Some of the doors have jammed and a shutter was blown off one morning, but otherwise we are all right. We had the rest centre open, which gave Helen plenty to do and kept her amused.

We went to Kensington today and bought Helen a costume. She looks very lovely in it, but there seem remarkably few coupons left. We also got some combs and I have one here for you if you need it. The papers have been full of letters from mothers complaining that they can buy no combs to send to their sons in Normandy. I don't know why people in France should need them more than people in Italy or Africa, but there it is.

That is all the news. I am so glad you are well and cheerful. We have had no doodles at all today – perhaps they have no time to bother about them any more. I must go and clean the kitchen.

With love from Aunt Molly

AUGUST 31, CHISWICK

My dearest Otto,

Anthea and Patience are still bathing a lot and both can almost dive. I have not seen much of them because my bicycle has disappeared. I relied on it so much for shopping[89] and now that and so much else is much harder and takes so much longer.

Today the weather made the children so cross I thought they had better have a static amusement for a change, so we went to the 1/- seats of the Commodore and saw a pleasant little romance called *It Happened One Sunday*.

I was slightly shattered after that because I went home to wash my hair, which was very dirty and on getting it clean discovered it had gone completely white at either side. The question now is shall

---

89   The shops were over half a mile away in Chiswick High Road.

I leave it permanently dirty to hide the white, or dye it, as suggested by Anthea, or go about with clean but mottled hair. Sister Alethe thinks it was Lawrence on his raft that turned it grey so suddenly, but I think it is entirely due to having no bicycle.

No, I think it unlikely you will get any leave before Christmas. Just a few people have had 36 hours, but they are either officers or people whose relations have been bombed out. The Americans who went over on D-Day have come back, but it looks as if they are staying here and will not be returning to the Continent. Anyway I am very thankful you are in Europe.

There is no more news and I have not done the shopping. Goodbye my son.

With love from Aunt Molly

SEPTEMBER 5, CHISWICK

My dearest Otto,

Here everything is as usual. No news, no bombs, nobody about – very quiet, as they say.

As it was raining hard yesterday and there was nothing to do, we went to the pictures. Helen and Anthea, who are romantic people, saw *Cover Girl*. Patience and I, who do not care for ROMANCE, saw *Gaslight*. It was a good drama with Charles Boyer as the would-be murderer and Ingrid Bergman as would-be murderee.

Last war everyone was longing for peace. This time I have already heard people say that they are frightened of it. Well, the great thing is to live from day to day and not look at the future. If we can get straight on with reconstruction it will be all right, but it is always difficult to get from one stage to another without a time lag.

Anthea and I went to the dentist today and returned rather the worse for the adventure. Cecily Heaton is getting very excited and threatens to join a school in Cheltenham and keep the boys with her while she works. Neville wants her to come back to The Hollies and I don't know if she wants to or not. They are both afraid of air raids and cannot make up their minds about anything but sending wires and fierce letters to each other. Cecily wrote to me, which is why I could not get your letter off yesterday. I had to invent a soothing and non-committal epistle in reply. Cecily, being Irish, gets so excited about things. On the other hand the English, because they have not much excitement in themselves – unlike the Irish and French and Italians – always want it going on outside. That is one reason why some people think it will be difficult getting people to settle down after the war. They have been so used to real excitement, they will not easily be contented with the artificial sort, like racing and football, which kept them going before the war. On the other hand I read in the paper yesterday that the Women's Forces are demanding lessons in cooking and there is a sudden revival in the art of embroidery among the ATS. Now that the war is nearly over, they want to start 'settling down'.

There is no more news. I wonder if you were among the people filling lorries with clothes and food for Paris.

With love from Aunt Molly

SEPTEMBER 8, CHISWICK

My dearest Otto,

I can't think how you manage to compose such interesting letters in spite of the censor. I imagine the censoring of letters from France will soon end, because we all see the same papers and have the same wireless news. I was very glad to hear of the liberation of Brussels and that our people went in before anyone else. How excited Madame and Denese will be. The Belgians here in Chiswick have produced an enormous Belgian flag and hung it out.

You ask if I ever think of the future. After the last war no one did, this time people think of little else. The WRENS have been told they are to remain on for two years after the end of the war. Probably this will hold for most of the Services. Hans is getting me the Government White Paper on UNRRA[90], which should tell something of the plans for people going back to their own countries.

This will sound grim to you – and to a lot of other people, too

---

90   United Nations Relief and Rehabilitation Administration.

– but it really is less grim than the unemployment that would be caused by demobilising everyone at once directly the war is over. Have you thought out any plans? When I think about a stateless future for you and Irene I do panic. Months ago Irene's department at the BBC served notices on its employees stating their 'services would not be required directly the war is over".

I am sorry this letter is so disjointed. I started it in the garden and then it began to rain. The small marks on the sheet are rain, not tears. We all had to come in and now everyone is talking. Are you still sleeping in tents? You mention sitting outside a barn to write letters. I am glad you have got some boxes with which to make a bed, because being raised off the ground will prevent you from getting rheumatism. I must say it sounds uncomfortable all the same.

They say the blackout is to be gradually lifted, which means we shall not have to spend a lot of money on new blackout material this autumn. They have turned the factories where they made this stuff into factories for peacetime curtains. If they can change all war things into peace things as quickly it will mean plenty of employment.

I bought a nice little lady puppy the other day. We will be able to have a family next summer. I think she comes from the same stock as Bonny, but I must get his pedigree and register him with the kennel club. The Croasdells also have a Dax pup, but he is smooth, not rough-haired like Bonny. The Rae-Scotts have two bull terriers. They get £6 each for the pups in spite of not having registered them. I hope to get at least that much for my pups next year.

I do not think your rain in Normandy can beat what we have had here. Yesterday it simply poured all day. I have Anthea with a poisoned foot. It needs a lot of looking after.

Helen has gone to stay with a friend near Oxford and Lawrence is back at the farm. He returns on Monday. He has had a lovely time in spite of the weather. I am so glad you can hear a wireless. Next time when there is not so much noise I will write a proper letter.

If you get very tied up and find writing too difficult, ask Myra to ring me up and tell me you are all right. I can imagine how difficult it is to write.

With love from Aunt Molly

Sept 12th  CHISWICK VICARAGE
THE MALL W 4

My dearest Otto

Thank you for your last letter. I hope you will move on in
a short time, and not have to stay too long in one place. It is so much
more interesting moving about.    I think the weather seems pretty bad
everywhere.    Lawrence came back from camp yesterday, looking rather thin,
because he seems to have grown about an inch in the fortnight. He had a
lovely time in spite of the rain, and worked very hard. They had Italian
prisoners working on the land at some of the farms. They conversed with
them in a mixture of english, latin, and French, using all the musical
terms freely. It sounds odd, but they managed to understand each other.
Helen has gone to stay with a friend for a week. She was very excited about
it, and I hope she will be able to go to a dance. They have dances at the
camps near, and as her friend's father is an air-marshal or something of the
sort they know a lot of the air-men.
Did I tell you that Lawrence wants to go into the army as a profession?
We are both disappointed with his decision, although as it has nothing to do
with anyone except himself we have not said so.    I must say my Father and
Dick, both english regulars, and Lawrence, U.S.regular, all loved the life
Lawrence wants to travel and see things and do exciting things, and the
army  is the obovious and easyest thing to go into if you feel like this.
On the other hand  all the army people I have known (regulars I mean) have
been very very nice, and kind and very good, but inclined to be dull, and
very narrow in their outlook. This is not their faults, but due to living
in a very small comurity, all of whom know one-and-other, and all of whom
have exactly the same ideas about all the things they do. Anyway there
it is and it remains to be seen what happens to any of us whatever our own
plans may be for the future.
Our new puppy is sweet, It is very wriggley and always on the move. The
Croasdells have a shiny black pup (a dax too) almost exactly the same age,
and they play together very nicely. I must say there is something very
attractive in the short coated Dax pups, but they are not nearly so nice
when they get older. They grow very fat.
Last week we heard such a lot of guns from France. It was just as we
used to hear them in the last war. We read in the papers that it was the
Canadians. I wonder what it sounds like in France when there is a great
battle raging a few miles off. I think the whole country must be incred-
ably noisy. Mrs Lugrin the hairdresser's wife (who's husband is dutch
by the way not Italian) is very thrilled because th  town where a lot of
her relations live, and where she herself lived for some time, is liberat
Anthea's foot is better. We went to do some shopping today, to get the
little girls ready for school. Eloise is taking Lawrence and Patience to
the Chiswick Empire tonight. After the performance they go back to his
flat and have a wonderful dinner, ending with coffee, and finishing up
with tea at about 10-30 before they come home. Very bad for them but
enjoyable. Eloise being a sailour can do most things, and even bottles
his own fruitand is a good cook, as well as being able to darn socks in
the approved fashion for sailours. I like to contemplate all you hundreds
of young men in France and Belgian darning your socks and doing your washing and generally being trained as perfect husbands of the future.
With love from

*A letter of September 12, 1944.*

The evening of September 8, Chiswick receives the first German V2 rocket launched at England. The 13-ton missile, moving too fast for radar detection, lands in Staveley Road, destroying 25 houses and damaging over 650 dwellings. The impact creates a crater 40 feet across and 20 feet deep and the explosion is heard as far away as Westminster. Three people are killed and 24 injured. In the next 10 days, 25 more V2s land in London and on November 10 Churchill says, "We are under attack again". London endures more V2s until the end of March 1945. Any letter Molly may have written about the incident has not survived.

SEPTEMBER 12, CHISWICK

My dearest Otto,

I hope you will move on in a short time and not have to stay too long in one place. It is so much more interesting moving about. I think the weather seems pretty bad everywhere. Lawrence returned from the farm yesterday looking rather thin. He seems to have grown about an inch in the fortnight. He had a lovely time in spite of the rain and worked very hard. There were some Italian prisoners working the land and Lawrence conversed with them in a mixture of English, Latin, French and musical terms. It sounds odd, but they managed to understand each other.

Did I tell you that Lawrence wants to go into the Army as a profession? Teddy and I are both disappointed with his decision, though as it has nothing to do with anyone except Lawrence we have not said so. I must say my father and Dick, both English Regulars, loved the life. Lawrence wants to travel and do exciting things and the Army is the obvious and easiest thing to go into if you feel like this. On the other hand all the Army people I have known (Regulars, I mean) have been very nice and kind and good, but inclined to be dull and very narrow in their outlook. This is not their fault, but due to living in a very small community where they all know one another and have exactly the same ideas about all the things they do.

Our new puppy is very sweet, very wriggly and always on the move. She plays very nicely with the Croasdell's shiny black Dax. I must say there is something very attractive in the short-coated Dax pups, but they are not nearly so nice when they get older. They grow very fat.

Last week we heard such a lot of guns from France, it was just as we used to hear them in the last war. We read in the papers that it was the Canadians. I wonder what it sounds like in France when there is a great battle raging a few miles off. The hairdresser's French wife is thrilled because the town where she lived is now liberated.

We went to do some shopping today to get the little girls ready for school. Blois Johnson is taking Lawrence and Patience to the Chiswick Empire tonight. After the performance they go back to his flat and have a wonderful dinner, ending with coffee at 10.30. It will be very bad for them but enjoyable. Blois, being a sailor, can do most things. He is a good cook – he even bottles his own fruit – and can darn socks in the approved fashion for sailors. I like to contemplate all you hundreds of young men in France and Belgium darning your socks and doing your washing and generally being trained as perfect husbands of the future.

With love from Aunt Molly

SEPTEMBER 16, CHISWICK

My dearest Otto,

I am writing this now while the house is quiet. Lawrence and Patience have sold one of the hens to the Owens. The butcher has killed it and they are all busy plucking it on the lawn. It never laid any eggs, but had some curious symptoms so they wrote to a poultry paper about it. The answer was that the hen should be killed at once before she died on her own.

Helen is very busy ironing a dress as she is going out with Roy, one of Mrs Volkov's medical students. They are making for Richmond, where they intend boating, having tea, supper and dancing. Roy is very respectable and I feel he is quite safe.

Did I tell you about the puppy? She has long floppy ears and feet as large as those of a policeman. She is greyish on top, with light brown ears and a diamond-shaped patch where her tail comes from her body, which makes her look as if she is wagging all over when her tail moves from side to side. She has had several differences of opinion with Dinah and now has a black eye as a result of the last of these.

We went to see *The Song of Bernadette* last week at the Gaumont[91]. Jennifer Jones is very good. I thought it was all a bit dark and dreary, but no one else did so perhaps I was just extra tired and could not appreciate it properly. I wish they would send *A Canterbury Tale* to Normandy, though I think what you really need is *Cover Girl*.

Anthea's foot is still bad. She poisoned it by hitting it on a bicycle pedal. We are constantly applying Kaolin poultice and she is now having ultraviolet ray treatment, which does seem to do it good. I hope she will be able to go back to school on Tuesday. It is horrid having to go back late, when everyone else has settled in and started work.

We have not heard about Helen's School Cert. yet. They are very late with them this year. Tom and Mary Nelson's daughter Bett, who has never been known to pass anything in her life before, got through first shot with a credit for history, which is her weakest subject. The Nelsons are very pleased. It looks as if Hans will get his extension from the Poly, so he is staying on with us.

Did I tell you that Teddy and I have moved the bedrooms round and we now sleep overlooking the river? Lawrence is in our room, Patience at the end of the passage and Anthea in the little blue room. Helen has been staying with a friend near Oxford and having a lovely time going to dances with airmen. The family are in a small cottage without a bath and on Friday nights they heat up the copper and bathe in the real old-fashioned way.

With love from Aunt Molly

---

91    The Gaumont Palace opened in 1932 as a cinema with 3,500 seats. It is now the Hammersmith Apollo, a concert venue.

My dearest Otto,

Helen's evening out with Roy last Saturday was a success. They started off with a film, then went to a Chinese restaurant and danced, then went on all over the place in a taxi. There was another boy and girl with them. They enjoyed it very much and Roy used up all his money so he will have to stay in and work all the week through to make up.

We are all slightly depressed because Helen has failed her School Certificate: four failures and two credits. She could try again, but four failures are too many to cope with. I must try to look out for things that can be done without a Cert.

We duly 'dimmed out'[92] last night and directly we had finished had an air-raid warning, so had to black out instead. However nothing came of the warning after all. The dim-out seems very much the same as the black-out but of course it sounds nicer.

I have tried to get magazines to send to you, but unless they are ones that are already ordered one cannot get them. We see pictures of the French villages, dreadful pictures and it makes one quite ashamed of complaining about a few silly bombs when one realises what the bombs and shells and fighting must have been like for those poor peasants. We are lucky in England. We can never be grateful enough for those 20 miles of water round our coast.

Goodbye little son.

With love from Aunt Molly

My dearest Otto,

Lawrence and Anthea went back to school yesterday. It was hectic and I feel like a very thin rag. Lawrence goes all scatty for the last three days of the holidays and not only forgets everything

---

92    Towards the end of the war, black-out restrictions were eased, allowing for outdoor light with the dimness of moonlight. In the event of an air raid, the 'dim-out' would revert to a total black-out.

he should remember himself, but also everything that anyone else reminds him of. It is awful. Now wherever I look, I find things that have been left behind, starting with Patience's washing materials and Anthea's stamp book.

Hans has a streaming cold and the beginning of a sty in his eye. He has started his last term at the Poly and has eight weeks in which to mug up his exam stuff again. Tomorrow he is taking Helen to supper at the Salad Bowl (his favourite eating place) and to see Bing Crosby in *Going My Way*, which is supposed to be BC's masterpiece. That is the day before she goes back to school.

I am afraid the paratroops that landed in Holland had a very rough time, poor things[93]. It is so cold here, we have had to give up summer frocks already.

Cecily Heaton is now working at a Cheltenham school where her baby, Martin, is in the pre-pre-preparation department and Nick in the pre-preparation department. Neville is with us as usual for supper and is slightly less shy than he used to be. I think the children have done him good.

With love from Aunt Molly

SEPTEMBER 25, CHISWICK

My dearest Otto,

I hear married men are to be 'demobbed' first. I always said you should get married. It is a pity you are in Normandy where the girls are short and dark. If you had been sent to Norway you might have picked up a very suitable tall and beautiful young Vikingess with eyes the colour of a fjord at night and long plaits of hair like ripe corn in the sunlight.

Helen goes to school today. I am having to take Puppy, now called Greeta, down to say goodbye to her because Puppy is in the process of being trained and cannot be left alone.

---

93  An unsuccessful Allied assault on the Netherlands disappointed hopes to end the war by Christmas.

Dinah's grey kitten suddenly seized and mauled the *Spectator* I am sending you, which is why it is torn. Teddy is away for three nights. Irene comes back on Thursday. Helen has seized the typewriter.

With love from Aunt Molly

OCTOBER 7, CHISWICK

My dearest Otto,

We had our parish party at the Hall last night. There were some stalls and it rather degraded into a sale instead of being a party. Also we had two sirens in the middle of it, so Mrs Hay, who would have played for the dancing, never came along. John Townsend was there, having just returned from Brussels. He is no longer fighting but pilots people about in planes as a sort of superior and highly paid aerial taxi driver. He brought some grapes back with him and we are all eating them now. What I remembered of grapes six years ago was so wonderful, but now, I am sorry to say, I find that like everything else they are just nice – very nice – but no more. We brought Neville Heaton with us, who nearly died of shyness until I introduced him to another civil servant and then they both unbent and became slightly human. I wonder what people like fighter pilots will do after the war. I think John is pretty typical, because he looks exactly like the airmen one sees in pictures in the papers and I can't think how such completely undisciplined people can fit into any normal life.

Another neighbour, John Davis (rear gunner) is also in Brussels. He has been home to say goodbye for the last time about once every fortnight for the last three months and now at last has gone. One of the Sisters made a dreadful mistake because by way of cheering up his mother, she remarked brightly that probably the war would be over before John had seen any fighting. This caused mortal offence as Mrs Davis considers that John IS the war and thinks that it is due to him alone that the Germans have been held at bay for so long.

I wanted to go up to town this afternoon and try to get a returned seat for *Peer Gynt* but spent half an hour in the dogmeat queue instead. Anyway there is such a lot to do before going away. Teddy and I are taking a trip, I will tell you more later.

With love from Aunt Molly

My dearest Otto,

Teddy and I are in Cheltenham and I am writing this in the hotel garden. It is nice and clean, not all dirty and dilapidated like London. They had one bomb at the beginning of the war and are immensely pleased with their war damage and are keeping it for the inspection of future generations. The shops here are very good. I easily bought Greeta a collar, which we could not find in London. I am thinking of buying a hat. It is the only thing one can get without coupons and so far all those are destined for Lawrence's shirts.

We went over the Ladies' College this morning (i.e. the girls' school) and this afternoon are going to tea with someone who lives in the country. I am looking forward to seeing the country, as even in town the trees are so lovely, all changing colour.

There is something important I want to tell you. I will let you know about it next week. It will be told to the family then, when we have decided everything.

With love from Aunt Molly


**Edward and Molly travel on from Cheltenham to Peterborough, where he is offered a residentiary canonry at Peterborough Cathedral. The job search at last ended, Molly is now temporarily in Peterborough making arrangements to move there at the end of the year.**


OCTOBER 15, PETERBOROUGH

My dearest Otto,

We are leaving Chiswick and coming here to Peterborough and I am afraid it will make your leaves difficult. They will not be a proper rest as they should be. Also, from the letters you wrote when posted here in 1942, I do not think you will like this town. If the Dean of St Paul's had moved, Teddy might have taken his place. As it was, the Dean would not take the job offered to him, so that was that. Teddy will be Canon and education officer for the diocese. It will take him all over the place, which he will love. Peterborough is big and full of Americans. People don't 'call' now and I see no way of the children's getting to know any other young people.

With love from Aunt Molly

My dearest Otto,

I understand why you do not like Peterborough. It is a small and incredibly dull town. There is one main street up which American soldiers and shop girls all walk arm in arm and then turn round and walk back again. There are a few Italian prisoners and a few Poles and no English people (except the girls). All the people in the street belong to the same age group and do the same thing. They are all also dressed exactly alike and all do their hair in the same way, so the impression one gets is of a well-drilled regiment of both sexes on the march.

And then one turns off from the main street and through the Cathedral arch into another world. It is very peaceful and green, with the wonderful Cathedral standing very still like a great wood of fossil trees in the centre. Our house is tucked behind, very old and quiet, built under the arches of what was the monks' dining hall.

There are some other very old houses all round. I think they must be occupied, but one never sees anyone coming out of them. All the time we were there we saw neither a dog nor a cat.

I am enclosing a sketch and hope the censor will pass it and not think it is a camouflaged plan for a gun site. The house is lovely, though when the Dean showed us over I could not think why he tried to head me off from looking at the kitchen. When at last I did break in I almost burst into tears. It is about four times as large as the one I have now, with all sorts of out-sheds round and no way of converting it. There are only five bedrooms and they are all huge, so large that our biggest carpets at the Vicarage (drawing-room and study) will look like mats on the floors. Anthea and Patience are having a room between them and Helen and Lawrence rooms to themselves. Teddy and I are having a panelled room and there is one great one in which to put people staying. I will have two beds and a divan in there and the drawing-room carpet on the floor. The archways from the old refectory come in to this room through the wall, also into the dining room and the bathroom. As usual the 'domestic offices' of the house are conspicuous by their absence. We have a bath that is obviously an afterthought and later still the people living in the house seem to have decided it would be a good thing to have a lavatory. They plunged wildly and put in three. One is in the bathroom, which is most inconvenient and the other two are scattered about the garden.

The Precincts seem a very odd place. We stayed in the town over the weekend and went round to visit the Bishop, the Archdeacon and the Canons but were not even offered a cup of coffee during that time. They were very vague as to the nationality of the soldiers in some of the Precinct's houses but thought they might be Poles or Czechs. Actually they are Poles and look very nice. To my mind they are one of the few bright spots in the place. At least they smile and say "good morning" and seem pleased to see one.

The Dean is very nice. He is the baby of the place, only five years older than Teddy. He told us rather pathetically that all the other deans, bishops and canons have had two wives. The late organist also had two wives, only he decided to have two at one time so had to go. He (the Dean) has no wife at all.

I think Helen may get to know some Americans because she belongs to the right age group. I wish I could get to know some and find out why there is something so fundamentally different in a young American and a young European. However I cannot ever do this because being a middle-aged lady, for them I do not exist.

With love from Aunt Molly

OCTOBER 20, CHISWICK

My dearest Otto,

Here we are back again in Chiswick. It is all rather difficult. Carpets are coming up and curtains down and furniture is being shoved about. Everyone seems ill in the parish and needs visiting and I am starting a group of young married women. Myra is coming to stay for the weekend, which will be lovely. She said she was bringing a meat ration, so on the strength of that I asked a couple to lunch and then when Neville got home I found he had given all his rations for a fortnight to Cecily over the weekend. He has no meat or margarine, which cancels out Myra's meat that the couple are going to devour on Saturday. I suppose I shall be able to think of something else for them in time. Poor Myra does not know that she is destined to help me mend the study carpet. Actually she does not know we are leaving. I have not told her or Irene, as it was too much trouble to write an extra letter and too involved to explain over the telephone.

I sent you some cigarettes yesterday and hope they will arrive. It is getting so cold and dark and they are the only comforting things I could think of. I never sent them before because I consider you smoke too much anyway and thought it should not be encouraged.

This is a very dull domestic letter. I am sorry, but there is little to say. Tell me if you want any warm things sent out.

With love from Aunt Molly

OCTOBER 25, CHISWICK

My dearest Otto,

On re-reading your last letter in a good light, I see it is a 'writing' not a 'washing' pad that you need. I could not imagine why you objected to washing with something with lines on it. Anyway I sent you two, because they seemed so very small. I hope they will do. Also I sent line-less washing things – face flannels, or whatever you call them. They were wound round the torch Myra bought for you. There are no torches in London but anywhere else is full of them.

We did an interesting thing last Sunday. Teddy preached at the Lincoln's Inn Chapel and we lunched at their Great Hall after. The chapel has great black oak pews, very high so no one can see over and in the days when services lasted hours and hours I think people went to sleep or played cards quite comfortably during the prayers. The pulpit is very high and they would have had to sit up during the sermon because the parson could see into all the pews. All the people in church were 'benchers', that is to say senior barristers or judges (they included two Indian ladies) and most of them came on to lunch after as they mostly lived out of town. We had a wonderful lunch and it almost seemed wrong to eat so much. They all sat to drink the King's health because Charles II had dined there one time when everyone was so tipsy they could not stand, so he gave them permission to drink to him sitting in future. It was like getting into another world, going there and being among people whose life is completely different to one's own. I only heard one person mention the Poles and she was an outsider and an authoress and I felt they were really just 'copy' to her. Being there, one could hardly believe we are at war, with all its cruelty, coldness, dirt and horror.

It is cold and wet and St Luke's Little Summer is as much a washout in England as it is in France.

This house looks awful, with very few carpets and practically no curtains. When the siren goes we have to leave the dining room carrying our food and eat in the gloom of the study. The top of the shutters in the dining room do not fit and while the curtains were up there was sufficient dim-out. Now they are down there is a great streak of light unshaded.

We have had a Dutchman who looks like a member of the Royal Family in disguise mending all the windows all over the house that have been broken by our Patience during the last 10 years. The little girls come back for half-term next week. Irene also comes. Myra and I mended the study carpet fairly successfully and got very dirty in the process.

With love from Aunt Molly


OCTOBER 27, CHISWICK

My dearest Otto,

Isn't it dreadful about the death of the Archbishop of Canterbury?[94] Everyone had built such high hopes for him. He was one of the few

---

94  William Temple died October 26, 1944. He had visited Normandy during the June invasion as the first Archbishop of Canterbury to go into battle since the Middle Ages.

people left over from the slaughter of the last war and there is no one to take his place.

Irene and I squeezed ourselves into *Peer Gynt* yesterday as her 21st birthday present. It is wonderful, but frightfully odd. Ralph Richardson was Peer, a very difficult part to act and he was on the whole time.

I am trying to get rid of things like dead bicycles and live kittens without much success. There is a 'ceiling' on the price of second-hand cycles, so shops will not buy them because they take so much time to repair they are not worthwhile re-selling. Lawrence and I took the body of that old pram that had been left in the garden by the Belgians three years ago and dumped it late one evening in the waste ground behind the old schoolroom. I shall have to do the same with the bicycles.

I will try to see *Richard III* before leaving London, as I think I shall not see another play for years after we leave. It is a pity in a way, but when one lives in a place, one never makes the best of it. I should have seen so many more productions while here and gone to more concerts. As it was, the concerts always clashed with Sunday school and the theatres seemed a long way off and cost a lot. One thing I am glad of is that I have walked all over the City and know it pretty well – also the Law Courts, all round Westminster, up the Parks and along the Embankment. These places are fascinating to me. The last place I explored was Houndsditch, while waiting for a train at Liverpool Street. It's so different to the rest of London.

I think when this is all over we will probably look back and be sorry we have not known more of the world while we had the chance. Perhaps it will be possible to rush around and see some more as a 'disembodied spirit'. I hope I shall be able to see Kashmir when I have left this world, because I have always longed to go there and I shall never do so now[95].

With love from Aunt Molly

---

95   Molly does visit Kashmir decades later.

My dearest Otto,

Patience and Anthea have been home for half term and done a lot of their packing up. Having them was lovely for me, but not very good for the children as they get so excited and tired and do not get to bed at the proper time. They went round and said goodbye to several people.

I must stop now as an enormous tramp has come in for a "drop of tea" and I don't want to leave him alone in the kitchen for too long. I meant to tell you last time I wrote that Alice came to see us again. The priest she worked for is going to India, so she will have to look for more work. This will not be hard to find as there is plenty of work for any 'domestic help'. I hope to get a daily in Peterborough to do the housework so I only have the cooking.

Do take care of yourself.

With love from Aunt Molly

**Otto is now in Belgium.**

My dearest Otto,

I want to send you a Christmas cake but I am sure it would arrive a heap of ruins, having been sat on by the postman, the censor and the man at the customs. Now what I will do in about ten days is send you the extra rations we are all getting for Christmas. You can present them to your landlady and ask her to make a cake or a pudding and let you have a large piece of whatever it is. As there is a shortage of fuel, baking may not be possible. Can you produce enough Flemish to explain this? Would you like a Flemish dictionary if I see one about? Though it is very unlikely I shall.

There is no news here except that Greeta is ill, with pains for apparently no reason in her inside. I took her to the vet and she has to live on Benger's invalid food for four days.

The Sisters at St Denys Cottage heard from Madame the other day. She said she was returning quite soon to Belgium. I will try to get her address. You might pop in and see her, only they are in the French-speaking district, which must be the other end of the country.

Teddy went to Westminster Abbey to Temple's memorial service. He said it was a wonderful sight. The canons wore the black and gold copes that had been made for the funeral of Charles II. He went with a friend to represent the Anglo and Eastern Orthodox churches. They had Americans in front of them and a wonderful-looking man with long gold hair came in and announced himself to the usher, "I am the Swedish Church!"

With love from Aunt Molly

P.S. Can your Belgians get coffee? It is un-rationed here and I could send some.

NOVEMBER 6, CHISWICK

My dearest Otto,

I was very disappointed to find I am not allowed to send you food. I think it is too bad. Apparently there has been a regular snowstorm of letters to the *Daily Mail* (including one from Miss Shaw) asking why we are not allowed to send our extra Christmas ration to Europe if we want to.

I love getting your letters about Belgium. Here in England we seem so safe, fat and well-fed and so far from everything it is rather depressing. We can't do anything and it makes one feel useless and ineffectual. We know someone who is a British Army Chaplain in Paris, a very nice man. He is helping with British internees who are coming out of camps. I should like to do something like that, but of course I can't. Somehow it does not feel quite so bad if I have you on the spot and able to help people, even if it is only a few individuals. I know you will always help anyone who needs it.

Our house is awful. We have no stair carpets now and everything is incredibly dirty. We always manage to move house in mid-winter, which is the worst time. When the carpets came up, we realised how the old house had been racketed by the bombing. The nails in the floors were all sticking up a quarter of an inch above the wood. We used to feel the house heave and come to rest again like a ship when the bombs came near and on several occasions it did not settle again quite straight. The doors on one side (generally the church side) jammed and had to be taken off and planed down again.

Did I tell you I am going to see Lawrence at Marlborough at the end of the month? He is being confirmed, so I shall go down for the weekend. I was very much afraid I would not be able to go because there seemed nowhere to be put up, but in the end Lawrence found a place just outside the town. I am looking forward to it most awfully. I shall return right in the middle of the move. It commences at 9 am and I get back about 12.

*When removing the stair carpet, Molly discovered all the tacks had been lifted up by the vibration of bomb explosions.*

I have been hearing much more cheering things about Peterborough lately. Apparently the inhabitants do not acknowledge the babble of Americans and tourists in their midst. They are just 'things' going on on top – sort of growths as it were. There are nice people living in farms and houses round and they all come in to the town to do their shopping. Anyway from the children's point of view there cannot be fewer people of their own age to know there than there are here.

Did I tell you that my eyes suddenly stopped working and I am having to wear glasses? I have ordered specs with sort of transparent rims. I hope to do a lot more reading when I get them. I have just finished a book called *The Rains Came*, which is about white and Indian people in an Indian state. It is well-written and vivid, but all the people have sex complexes. It seems odd that in such a small place there should be so many people who need the administrations of a trained psychologist. The people who are normal the author looks upon as completely abnormal and cannot understand at all himself.

With love from Aunt Molly

NOVEMBER 10, CHISWICK

My dearest Otto,

It was so cold and dirty here yesterday and Teddy was out all day, so I went to London on the chance of getting into *Richard III* and actually got an excellent seat in the gallery without a wait. Laurence Olivier was Richard. It is a bit of an adventure making your hero such a complete villain.

Is Hitler dead[96]? People seem to think he is. There are little excited bits about it every now and again in the papers. I wonder if it is wrong to hope he died of an agonising screaming cancer and that he, like Richard, saw in his dreams the spirits of those he murdered sighing gently past him and cursing him. I always think it is best to stick to the Bible and say "Vengeance is mine saith the

---

96   Hitler committed suicide six months later, in April 1945.

Lord and I will repay it." I think if people start trying to repay it themselves, they just drag themselves down and the worst they can do is to kill a man, which is too easy.

This is a horrid end to a letter. It is theories running loose again so I had better stop.

With love from Aunt Molly

My dearest Otto,

The house is in an incredible muddle. I scrubbed and shut up the larder yesterday and now all the food that is not packed is in the kitchen hiding from the cats. The things I think we will not need I pack up and of course we always want them in the end so I am constantly unpacking neat parcels and re-packing them not so neatly.

Then a few days ago Mr Elmslie fell over (or into, I am not sure which) a grave and sprained his ankle. Most of us when we do this bandage up the ankle and hobble about for a few days. Not so our Stewart. He had to go away for 10 days' holiday (two Sundays!) and the result is that I now have Teddy in bed, collapsed from overwork. I insisted on his staying in bed and shutting the church today. He is better now, but no one can do everything and unless Stewart returns soon, it will happen again. I must say I am longing now to get away from here, it is all too difficult. Patience and Anthea seem to have changed the day when they break up. It will complicate matters as they will arrive later than Helen instead of on the same day.

Greeta is well again. We think she sits in the study grate and chews coke and it upsets her insides. She is so sweet, I wish you could see her. She can curl into quite a tight compact ball in spite of being so long and pulled-out in her normal state. She is also very cuddly, like a baby.

I sent you some soap the other day. I have heaps and if you want more, let me know. I am allowed to send it so my conscience is quite limpid on this subject – like a clear and crystal stream.

George came to see us last night after almost a year away. He has been all over Europe and says he wants to become a missionary. We advised him to go with an organisation because he was talking of going by himself, which is a terrifying thought. George is such a darling but somehow he has not got a very strong hold on life and I always feel he might slip out very easily if anything happened. I do not think he has ever enjoyed it very much.

The hen I gave to the Sisters seems to be dying. I took two of Neville's hens to the butcher today. I now have a cock, two cats and a new addition, a Belgian hare, to deal with. Flopsy the hare has had the run of the house. She is so sweet I do not want to kill her.

By the way there will be some more socks coming along at the beginning of January. I thought I would wait till after the Christmas rush and think you will have had the others three months by then.

With love from Aunt Molly

NOVEMBER 25, CHISWICK

My dearest Otto,

We are going round saying goodbye to people. I am feeling each day more and more like a Russian off for a long term to Siberia. I found a rusty pair of skates and have packed them. Helen has been suspiciously quiet about her studies all term, except for at the beginning, when she wrote and told me brightly that she was giving up French. I disapprove of this. One hardly ever uses it in England, but it is nice to know a little. At the beginning of each war my French comes to life again just enough to enable me to explain necessities to Belgian refugees.

With love from Aunt Molly

My dearest Otto,

I am writing this at the hotel sitting up in bed very grandly because breakfast is not till nine o'clock. I arrived yesterday and got a seat all the way because I started from home at about 7 am. Only the people who were waiting long before the Reading train came in got seats. At Savernake we all got out and finished the journey through the forest by bus. In theory this should have been lovely. In practice we saw only the people we were squashed up against. I said I would meet Lawrence at the principal pub and found it occupied by Americans. I left my grip there and met Lawrence at the school. He is very thin and anyway his arms have grown inches and I will have to let down the sleeves of his new coat.

Everyone at the college has German measles and I am afraid there is little chance of his escaping. In the summer the town had it so badly that all the schools shut. It is not a serious complaint (not so bad as flu) but is 'notifiable', which means you are in quarantine for it. Two people in his room went down with it last night. It is a bother as he will have to stay at school if he gets it. I am staying in a small house on one of the Marlborough hills. The position is lovely and the view wonderful but oh-so-cold. I feel I am preparing for Peterborough, where they tell me the wind sweeps straight across from the Steppes of Russia.

Lawrence is being confirmed this morning. He is coming here for breakfast and lunch and we will have tea in the town and I'll get a train back at 5.30. We have evacuated the Vicarage, which has been seized by furniture packers and are with the Heatons at The Hollies for the next three days. Please don't forget to write to THE PRECINCTS, PETERBOROUGH. I know most of the letters sent to me from abroad will have to be forwarded for the next six months. I have told everyone, but some letters take so long. Those from my sisters in Kenya may not arrive at all.

There are not so many American troops round here now. I think most of them are going abroad, poor things. Winter warfare must be ghastly. We had a lovely farewell party given by the parish on Friday.

With love from Aunt Molly

My dearest Otto,

The furniture has gone and we are here for the night. Neville is taking us to a theatre as a sort of farewell to London. Cecily is home now but has to return to the children's school in Cheltenham this afternoon.

I interviewed Lawrence's housemaster on Saturday. He holds a very dim view of the future for boys in general and for Lawrence in particular. When I had done with him, I was almost as scared about life after the war for Lawrence as I am for you. I think it is wrong to panic and shows a lack of faith. I think if one remains calm and holds on to the fact that there is special work that only can be done by special people and if one takes all openings that come, one will be guided into the right path.

Did I tell you that Hans passed his exam? He did not get honours, which he expected. I do not quite know how he missed honours, as he had no coursework to do, no one to compete with and all the special attention he wanted at the Poly. I suppose he is just not as clever as we all thought. He is joining the Army.

Greeta is ill again, which is complicating our move. I had to spend 1½ hours waiting at the vet with her this morning and she has to be given doses and forcibly fed with milk. The car is out again at last. Do you remember when we put it away 'for the duration' at Christmas five years ago? Teddy is so pleased to have it back. I wonder if you are pleased to be chopping down trees again. Will you come in under the scheme for leave, or is it only for the people who went out at the beginning? I hope my brother will get home soon from Africa. He has been away four years.

With love from Aunt Molly

My dearest Otto,

This is the most extraordinary place. It is almost fantastically lovely, like the scenery of an opera, the Cathedral outlined in front of the stars, the lights from windows glowing from the insides of mediaeval arches, the courtyards, hidden passages, old gardens and older houses. I have never felt so far from life and so nearly a ghost. I wonder what your reactions will be.

My poor little puppy got distemper. I had to let the vet put her to sleep. I shall never have another. She is the second little bitch I have lost. One gets so fond of them.

Our furniture arrived very late – today instead of yesterday – and then only two vans, not four. It has put us back and we will not be settled till next week. It is very cold here and the fuel shortage makes things difficult. The people who have been here for years save fuel violently through the summer to have enough in winter.

I hope a small parcel will arrive for you for Christmas. There will be no *Listener* this week as I can't get it. I will make some arrangement next week.

With love from Aunt Molly

DECEMBER 20, MINSTER PRECINCTS, PETERBOROUGH

My dearest Otto,

Life at the moment is one wild rush. Half of it consists in trying to get the curtains up successfully and half in children's clothes and washing things and the other half (which makes three halves to a whole) in doing things like cooking. The house is lovely and feels very peaceful and nice. The curtains fit most of the windows, but they fit very skimpily. On the other hand, if they did not fit at all there would have been no way of buying any, so we are frightfully lucky. Fortunately there is no black-out, so we can have transparent curtains.

The town is very good for shopping, with the exception of shoes and no one here seems able to mend them. Result: Anthea has to go about with a shoe with no heel.

Teddy is 'installed' tomorrow in the afternoon. Oddly enough, in the morning a master from Lawrence's prep school is being made a priest, so Lawrence will have to go to that too and will spend a busy day watching people being made things. After the instalment the Bishop is giving a party to all the people in the Precincts so we will get to know them. At least the Bishop is not doing it, but Mrs Blagden is. She is the

Bishop's second wife and was the headmistress of a large girls' school near here. She is frightfully kind and just like all schoolmistresses all over the world, very much on the spot and good at organising.

Irene descends on us in a few days' time and Miss Coverley after that, then Helen has a friend to stay. I wish they were not all coming so much in a heap but suppose it will be all right. I have just bought Lawrence a shirt. The idea is that he shall wear it till it is dirty, then go to bed for a couple of days while I wash and iron it and then begin all over again. We also got him a pair of pyjamas, as his have to descend to Patience because hers have to go to Anthea.

With love from Aunt Molly

DECEMBER 22, MINSTER PRECINCTS, PETERBOROUGH

My dearest Otto,

Uncle Edward was installed yesterday. We had a nice little service and then went to tea at the Blagdens', where we met most of the other Precinct dwellers. The most unusual of them all is Bishop Lang. He is brother to the late Archbishop and completely bats. The other day I saw him passing by the ruins of the washhouses and thought to myself, "Now I really have seen a ghost". He is very tall and thin, all in black wearing gaiters and apron and as he has no hair, he wears a skullcap. He really might have stepped out of almost any page of history. I think he is really nice to talk to but a bit alarming. To begin with, he will not behave like anyone else during a service but will sit when others stand and stand when others kneel and occasionally he disappears altogether in the stalls, which is very alarming if you are not prepared for it. Also, if you try to sit in the same row of seats as he sits in during a service, he orders you out and makes you sit somewhere else. Lawrence and old Mrs Blakeney [wife of Canon Blakeney] have both suffered from him in this respect so, when I see him anywhere, I always sit as far away from him as I can. The other people in the close are mostly very old, but quite nice. So many have lost sons in the war. I must stop now and finish the lunch.

With love from Aunt Molly

*The Bishop, Dean and Archdeacon
wore apron and gaiters.*

DECEMBER 25, MINSTER PRECINCTS, PETERBOROUGH

My dearest Otto,

This is my usual Christmas Day letter. I meant to write one so you would get it on the 25th, but failed. Thank you so much for the parcel, which arrived safely. Powder and pens, just what I needed. How did you know? They are such nice pens, too. Lawrence is having one because he lost his. The other I am keeping, but lending to Patience for the time being as she had hers stolen at school. She has put down her name for a pen at Smith's and will get one in a few months, so I shall have mine back then. Anyway I hope in a few weeks' time we will all have pens again, thanks to you.

It is very cold and foggy. Helen and I went to the Cathedral for morning service. They have two huge Christmas trees decorated by our children and the three sons of Archdeacon and Mrs Grimes. The trees look lovely, with lights on them and a Christmas crib in between. The Grimeses have given us 'Yule logs', which are a very good present in this climate. The three very tall Grimes boys brought them over on Christmas Eve.

The children and I attacked the garden yesterday. We were weeding and discussing the afterlife. I wonder why it is that when two or three people garden together this subject always comes up. We all rather like talking about it, because of course we know nothing about it and we can let our imaginations run riot. In the end I made a hole in my hand and have blisters all over the palm and the garden looks much the same as it did before. I want to get the ground clear so as to be able to plant fruit bushes as soon as possible in the spring.

I am sorry my Christmas parcel arrived so long before the day. The idea was that parcels were arrive in good time and to be kept back for handing out on the 25th. One woman wrote a furious letter saying her husband had been given his two months early. Anyway I am glad you had not got a lighter. All the things in the tin were suggested by a gentleman on the wireless. It was a help, as most of us had blank minds on the subject.

It was lovely to get a letter from you on Christmas morning. Dear son, this wishes you all the best happiness for the New Year. That is all I can wish you.

With love from Aunt Molly

# AFTERWORD

The move from wartime London in the Vicarage to Peterborough must have been a huge wrench for Molly, though our father was keen to have a change. For us children, by then adolescents, it was wonderful. On one side of Peterborough lay the vast, mysterious Fen country and on the other, the rambling, pale yellow Barnack stone villages. The great cathedral sat in the centre of the town, a gigantic, benign and beautiful presence.

Our house was in the cathedral grounds (the Precincts), built within the arches of the monks' dining hall, part of the remains of the sacked, pre-Reformation monastery. The house was altogether delightful but unmodernised. A tiny bathroom with a loo was the only concession to modernity. The kitchen was even more medieval than the one at Chiswick. Molly had to manage kitchen cupboards so deep that we never saw the backs of them. Our Belgian hare, Flopsy, came with us. She lived with us in the house but had a tiny enclosed garden leading out from the side of the hall.

Dinah, our black Manx cat, disappeared a week before we left the Vicarage and reappeared the day of departure, discovered sitting on a suitcase in the car. Molly had said she should probably put Dinah down because she never thought the little cat would cope with the change. Dinah must have overheard this comment and swiftly acted on it. Bonny took the move in his stride.

After a few days our mother began to get used to the very different atmosphere of Peterborough. With her love for and interest in people, she soon made friends with those living in the Precincts, the town and the country – a real mix of friends. Her house was often filled with people dropping in for a chat or a cup of tea. There was also an excellent repertory theatre.

Helen and Patience were married from the Cathedral. After National Service and Oxford, Lawrence married and was employed for most of his working life by the National Trust. I went to Chelsea School of Art in the early '50s and later also married.

Finally, after six or so years at Peterborough, Teddy and Molly left, first to Sudbury in Suffolk and later to Padbury in Bucks. Our father was going through a crisis in his spiritual life and a few years before his death he was received into the Roman Catholic Church. This meant his life as a C of E clergyman inevitably came to an end. It was a source of sadness for Molly, but Edward thoroughly enjoyed the remaining years of his life as a Catholic. They lived then in a dear little house in Yeoman's Row in Knightsbridge. After Edward's death, Molly had 15 years as a widow. She took a flat overlooking the back wall and trees of Kew Gardens and spent many hours in the gardens. My sisters and I were with her when she died, aged 75, at my house in London. Up to her death, Molly remained a vivid, loving, unselfish and very special friend to us all and to Otto.

Otto stayed in the Army until November 1946. His final posting was as an interpreter for the military government in Brunswick, Germany. Afterwards, he took a degree in history at Birkbeck College, University of London and taught history at various colleges of education. He married very happily and has two daughters.

*Lawrence with Dinah.*

# ACKNOWLEDGEMENTS

When Otto gave me my mother's correspondence 20 years ago, I had every intention of reading it through and choosing special letters to give us an idea of what life was like for a family living through the war in London. But the thousand pages proved too much, especially as they were typed or scribbled on sometimes tiny pieces of fragile paper. It was a monumental task. So after years of starts and stops, I thought of my friend in New York, the superb Cynthia Penney. Cynthia was a tower of strength as the editor, researcher, genealogist and project manager of Molly's letters. She came to love Molly and was able to discuss with me what should or should not be included. Her interest was for Molly's voice. The only thing we changed from the original letters was Molly's spelling. This is a pity, but it does make the reading so much easier. Nothing else is altered. Molly's easy flow was always crystal clear. My wish is that this extraordinary human being who worked so tirelessly and with such faith and energy will be remembered and loved by others who weren't able to meet her.

I would also like to thank my secretary, Barbara Linton, for all her help with the planning and management of this book for publication and her husband Peter and son Robert, who tirelessly transcribed all of the letters.

```
        My brain is so rusty I could almost hear it working. I am
going to another thing of the same sort all about Zionists soon. Can you
find out from your Zionists all about what they expect to do. I have a
friend who sends girls and boys out to Palestine to work on farms. she
has them trained first. I think it would be rather lovely to go there and
grow oranges with chickens underneath.
```

*One of Molly's typewritten letters.*

# APPENDIX 1

**Incidents caused by Enemy Action in the Borough of Brentford and Chiswick. Air Raid Precautions Records 1940-45.**

**Alerts**     1,216

**Casualties**  778 (78 fatal, 216 seriously injured, 484 minor)

**Missiles**

| | |
|---|---|
| Anti-aircraft shells – exploded | 45 |
| Anti-aircraft shells – unexploded | 31 |
| High explosive – exploded | 359 |
| High explosive – unexploded | 25 |
| High explosive – unexploded, later exploded | 8 |
| Incendiary bombs | 7,000-8,000 (very approximate) |
| Mines – parachute | 2 |
| Mines – type G magnetic | 1 |
| Oil bombs | 32 |
| Parachute bomb | 1 |
| Phosphorus incendiary bomb – exploded | 12 |
| Phosphorus incendiary bomb – unexploded | 27 |
| Shrapnel Causing Casualties | 6 |

Flying Bombs – V1    13 occurrences:
*Thames Rd, Ellesmere Rd, Prince's Ave, Boston Manor Rd (2), Cubitt's Yacht Basin, County Grammar School (3), Burlington Lane, Thornton Ave/Mayfield Ave, Homefield Rd/Chiswick Lane, Clayponds Ave, Ferry Lane, Apple Garth, Chestnut Ave, Hartington Rd, County, Staveley Road School, Chiswick Polytechnic, Bath Road*

Long-range rockets – V2    1 occurrence: *Staveley Road*

NUMBER OF OCCURRENCES    637

# APPENDIX 2

**WW2 TIMELINE 1939–1945**
**Events, military and domestic, that affected Molly and her family.**

## 1939

3 SEPTEMBER Britain and France declare war on Germany two days after Hitler invades Poland. German U-boats are soon attacking British naval convoys in the Atlantic, but Western Europe is quiet for eight months, leading the British to call this period the 'Phoney War'.

23 SEPTEMBER Petrol rationing begins in Britain, ending only in 1951, five years after the end of the war. Eventually coal, gas and electricity are also rationed.

## 1940

8 JANUARY Food rationing begins with restrictions on bacon, butter and sugar. Ration coupons or points are eventually required for meat, milk, tea, margarine, jam, cheese, rice, fresh and dried eggs, tinned fruit and vegetables, sweets, chocolate and biscuits. Food rationing does not end completely until July 1954.

9 APRIL Germany invades Denmark and Norway.

10 MAY Germany invades Holland, Belgium and France. Winston Churchill replaces Neville Chamberlain as Prime Minister.

27 MAY – 4 JUNE British and French troops pinned down on the north coast of France are evacuated from the port of Dunkirk. Britain assumes a German invasion of England is imminent.

10 JUNE  Italy declares war on Britain and France.

22 JUNE  France surrenders to Germany.

10 JULY  The Battle of Britain lasts throughout the summer and autumn, as British planes defend England from aerial attack. The RAF's resistance eventually compels Hitler to put his invasion plans for England on hold.

30 JULY  Molly's brother Dick is killed fighting Italian troops in Ethiopia.

7 SEPTEMBER  The first night of the London Blitz. The air raids continue until 11 May 1941.

27 SEPTEMBER  Germany, Italy and Japan sign a mutual-assistance agreement.

8 OCTOBER  German bombs ignite Church Wharf and flames threaten St Nicholas, the Vicarage and all of Church Street.

5 NOVEMBER  US President Franklin Delano Roosevelt is re-elected to an unprecedented third term.

29 DECEMBER  A major raid sets fire to the City of London, which St Paul's Cathedral survives.

## 1941

11 MARCH  Roosevelt signs the Lend-Lease Bill, providing war materiel to the Allies.

22 MARCH  Britain begins the conscription of women by registering all British females between the ages of 18 and 60

6 APRIL  Germany invades Greece and Yugoslavia.

16 APRIL  A bomb damages St Paul's Cathedral.

1 JUNE  Clothes rationing begins, lasting until 1949.

22 JUNE  Germany invades Russia.

14 AUGUST Roosevelt and Churchill announce the Atlantic Charter, establishing guidelines for post-war settlement.

2 DECEMBER  A new National Service Bill includes compulsory service for British women.

7 DECEMBER  Japan attacks Pearl Harbor, a major US naval base in Hawaii. The US and Great Britain declare war on Japan.

## 1942

1 FEBRUARY  Soap rationing begins, lasting until 1950.

15 FEBRUARY  Japan takes Singapore, a vital naval base.

26 MAY  Britain and Russia sign a mutual assistance agreement.

30 JULY  British civilians are no longer required to carry gas masks.

1 OCTOBER  All British women aged 20 – 45 are required to register for fire-watching.

4 NOVEMBER  German forces retreat from North Africa after The Second Battle of El Alamein.

## 1943

2 FEBRUARY  Germany surrenders the Russian city of Stalingrad.

12 MAY  Axis troops surrender in North Africa.

10 JULY  The Allies land in Sicily.

25 JULY Mussolini is ousted from power.

3 SEPTEMBER  The Allies land on the Italian mainland. The post-Mussolini government signs an armistice, which is announced on 8 September.

13 OCTOBER  Italy declares war on Germany after Hitler's troops invade in the north.

**1944**

27 JANUARY  A Russian victory ends Germany's 900-day siege of Leningrad (Saint Petersburg).

18 FEBRUARY  The 'Little Blitz' begins with renewed bomb attacks on England.

4 JUNE  The liberation of Rome.

6 JUNE  D Day, the landing of Allied troops on the beaches of Normandy, France.

13 JUNE  The first German V1 flying bomb lands in England and raids continue through October, with as many as 100 rockets launched per day.

15 AUGUST The Allies invade the south of France.

25 AUGUST  The liberation of Paris.

3 SEPTEMBER  The liberation of Brussels.

6 SEPTEMBER  Black-out restrictions in Great Britain are changed to allow a 'dim-out' on nights without air-raid warnings.

8 SEPTEMBER  The first V2 rocket to reach London lands in Chiswick. V2s are launched against England through March 1945.

13 OCTOBER The Allies occupy Athens.

**1945**

17 JANUARY Russian troops advancing on Berlin from the east take control of Warsaw.

7 MARCH Allied forces begin crossing the Rhine, advancing on Berlin from the west.

12 APRIL Franklin Roosevelt dies six months into an unprecedented fourth term as President. He is succeeded by Harry S Truman.

28 APRIL Mussolini is executed by Italian partisans.

30 APRIL Hitler commits suicide in Berlin.

7 MAY The unconditional surrender of Germany.

8 MAY VE Day (Victory in Europe).

26 JULY Clement Attlee replaces Winston Churchill as Prime Minister.

28 JULY Field Marshal Montgomery, a former resident of Chiswick, is honoured with the Freedom of Chiswick and a parade.

6 AUGUST A US plane drops an atomic bomb on Hiroshima, Japan.

9 AUGUST A US plane drops an atomic bomb on Nagasaki, Japan.

14 AUGUST President Truman announces Japan's unconditional surrender (signed September 2).

15 AUGUST VJ Day (Victory Over Japan) is celebrated as the end of the Second World War.

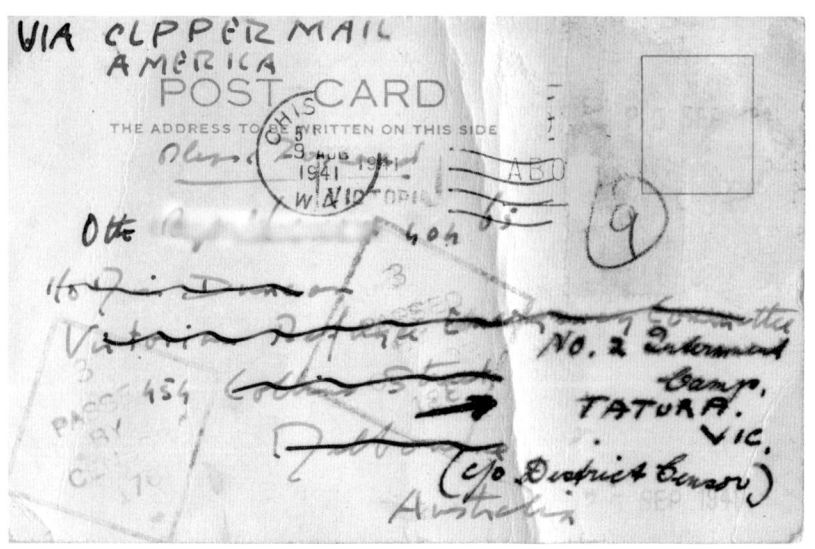

Chiswick Vicarage The Mall W4. *Dearest Otto*

We have applied for your release under agricultural "scheme".

We did not realise that your cable had taken a month to come till after Tyra received your letter. What I cabled to you in reply to your cable is what the Home Office had told us. Now a new application has been sent in. The Austrian Centre are doing it this time. Bloomsbury Ho. have not much hope, & Miss Duncan wrote to me — her letter crossed my cable to her — saying she did not think you could come home. Austrian Centre think it very possible. Of course a lot will depend on what happens to the war. Don't expect anything. I am just going to refuse to think about it all. Last time when we heard you were not coming back as a Pioneer it was too frightfully disappointing. They tell us that if you are released & returned home we will not know till you are on the way here. Miss Duncan says she will see you get clothes to travel in if you come back. I shall cable you this information, but there is nothing you can do. Just pray for the right thing to happen. All well. Very warm here. No raids —

*A postcard sent by Molly to Otto in Australia dated August 1941.*